Getting Started with ArcInfo

ArcInfo™ 8

Bob Booth

Contents

Getting to Know ArcInfo   1

Introduction   3

Conducting a GIS Project   57

8 Analyzing data   131

9 Presenting your results   165

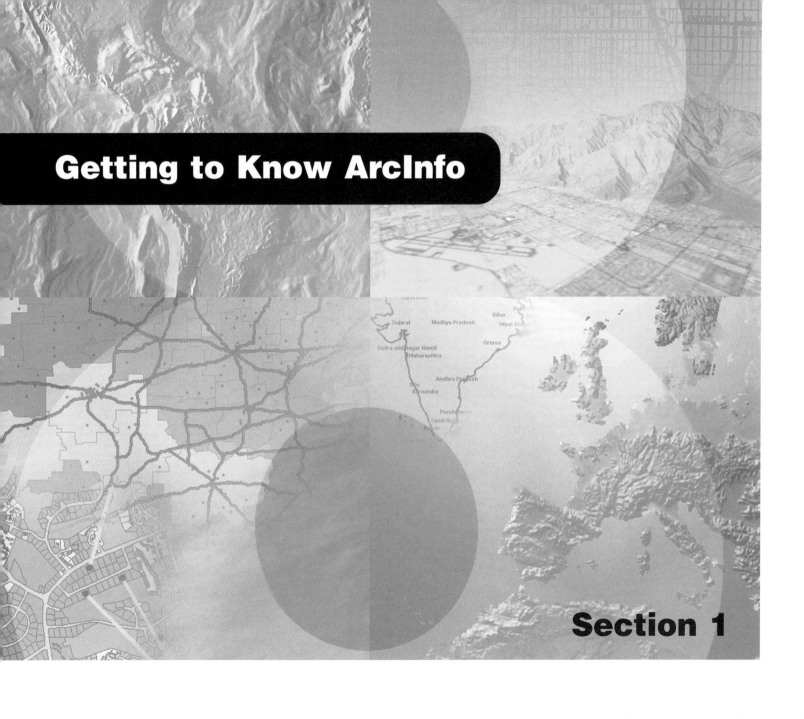

Getting to Know ArcInfo

Section 1

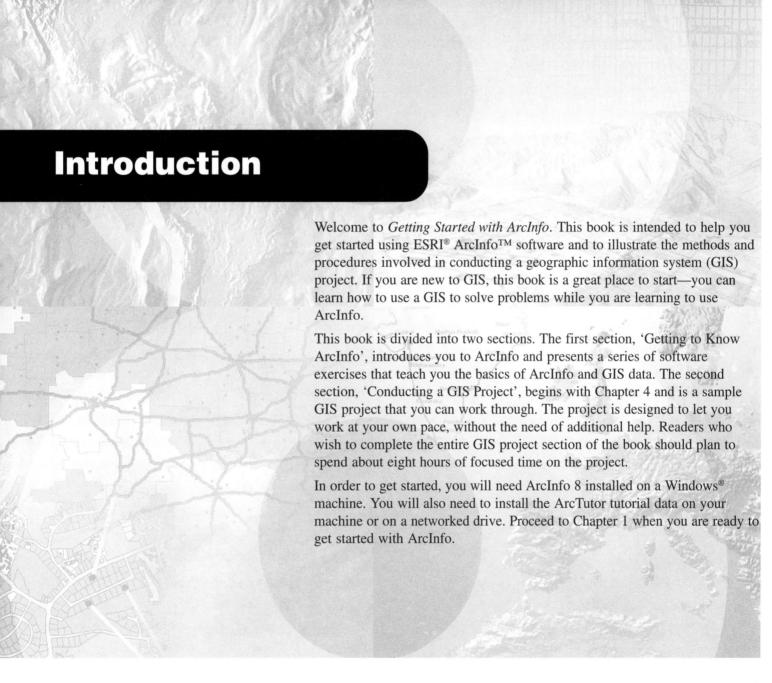

Introduction

Welcome to *Getting Started with ArcInfo*. This book is intended to help you get started using ESRI® ArcInfo™ software and to illustrate the methods and procedures involved in conducting a geographic information system (GIS) project. If you are new to GIS, this book is a great place to start—you can learn how to use a GIS to solve problems while you are learning to use ArcInfo.

This book is divided into two sections. The first section, 'Getting to Know ArcInfo', introduces you to ArcInfo and presents a series of software exercises that teach you the basics of ArcInfo and GIS data. The second section, 'Conducting a GIS Project', begins with Chapter 4 and is a sample GIS project that you can work through. The project is designed to let you work at your own pace, without the need of additional help. Readers who wish to complete the entire GIS project section of the book should plan to spend about eight hours of focused time on the project.

In order to get started, you will need ArcInfo 8 installed on a Windows® machine. You will also need to install the ArcTutor tutorial data on your machine or on a networked drive. Proceed to Chapter 1 when you are ready to get started with ArcInfo.

Welcome to ArcInfo

1

Welcome to ArcInfo, the leading software for professional GIS. You can do virtually any GIS job at any scale of complexity with ArcInfo, from conducting a single analysis project on your own to implementing a vast, multiuser, enterprisewide GIS for your organization.

Use this book to learn what GIS is all about, and in just a short time you can begin to apply ArcInfo for all of your GIS needs.

Today, GIS is used by thousands of different organizations and hundreds of thousands of individuals to access and manage fantastically varied sets of geographically related information.

In this chapter, you will find samples of real-world uses of ArcInfo, a brief discussion of the different ways that GIS is used, some examples of how ArcInfo lets you use central GIS functions, and finally, some directions for learning more about ArcInfo.

What can you do with ArcInfo?

A tax assessor's office produces land use maps for appraisers and planners.

An engineering department monitors the condition of roads and bridges and produces planning maps for natural disasters.

A water department finds the valves to isolate a ruptured water main.

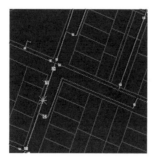

A transit department produces maps of bicycle paths for commuters.

A police department studies crime patterns to intelligently deploy its personnel and to monitor the effectiveness of neighborhood watch programs.

A wastewater department prioritizes areas for repairs after an earthquake.

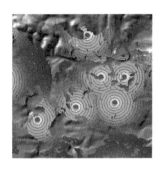

A telecommunication company studies the terrain to find locations for new cell phone antennae.

A hydrologist monitors water quality to protect public health.

A pipeline company finds the least-cost path for a new pipeline.

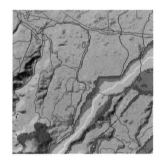

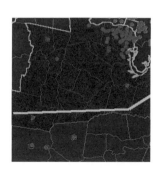

A biologist studies the impact of construction plans on a watershed.

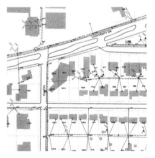

An electric utility models its circuits to minimize power loss and to plan the placement of new devices.

A meteorologist issues warnings for counties in the path of a severe storm.

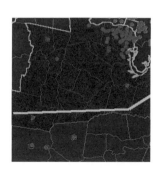

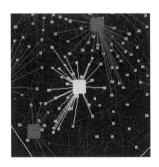

A business evaluates locations for new retail outlets by considering nearby concentrations of customers.

A police dispatcher finds the fastest route to an emergency.

An emergency management agency plans relief facilities by modeling demand and accessibility.

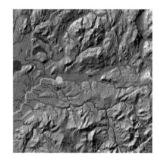

A water resource manager traces upstream to find the possible sources of a contaminant.

A fire fighting team predicts the spread of a forest fire, using terrain and weather data.

Unique projects to daily business

You can use ArcInfo in different ways, depending on the complexity of your needs.

Some people use ArcInfo primarily as a single-user mapping and analysis tool, usually in the context of a well-defined, finite project. This common use of ArcInfo is sometimes called project GIS. Other people use ArcInfo in a multiuser system designed to serve an organization's ongoing needs for geographic information. Multiuser GIS is sometimes divided into departmental and enterprise GIS, according to a system's level of complexity and integration with the day-to-day operation of an organization.

This book presents ArcInfo in the context of project GIS because a project is a good, self-contained way to explore a variety of basic GIS functions.

Project GIS

In a GIS analysis project, an analyst faces a variety of tasks that can be grouped into four basic steps.

The first step is to convert a question, such as "Where is the best place for a new building?" or "How many potential customers are near this store?", into a GIS database design and an analysis plan. This involves breaking the question into logical parts, identifying what layers of data will be needed to answer each part, and developing a strategy for combining the answers to each part of the question into a final answer.

The next step is to create a database that contains the geographic data required to answer the question. This may involve digitizing existing maps, obtaining and translating electronic data from a variety of sources and formats,

making sure the layers are of adequate quality for the task, making sure the layers are in the same coordinate system and will overlay correctly, and adding items to the data to track analysis result values. Personal workspaces of file-based data and personal geodatabases are used to organize project GIS geodatabases.

The next step is to analyze the data. This usually involves overlaying different layers, querying attributes and feature locations to answer each logical part of the question, storing the answers to the logical parts of the question, and retrieving and combining those answers to provide a complete answer to the question.

The final step in a project-based analysis is to communicate the results of the analysis, usually to people who do not use GIS and who have different levels of experience in dealing with maps. Maps, reports, and graphs are all used, often together, to communicate the answer to the question.

Multiuser GIS

In a multiuser GIS, people in an organization—from a few in a single office to hundreds in different branches—use the GIS in different ways to support their daily tasks.

Departmental GIS refers to systems developed within a single department to support a key function of the department. For example, a planning department might routinely use GIS to notify property owners of proposed zoning changes near their property.

A departmental GIS is usually managed within the department and often has specialists devoted to different tasks. For example, a department might have its own system administrator, digitizer, and GIS analyst. Departmental GIS is often customized to automate and streamline procedures. For example, a planning department could use a GIS application that finds the names and addresses of parcel owners within a designated area and automatically generates notification letters.

An enterprise GIS spans departments in an organization. These large systems support multiple functions of an organization, from daily business to strategic planning. An enterprise GIS is usually managed as a part of the organization's information technology infrastructure. For example, a city's enterprise GIS integrates the business functions of building and maintaining the city. The engineering department builds the infrastructure for a subdivision using the same geodatabase that the planning department and assessor use to do their jobs.

An organization's entire network becomes the platform for an enterprise GIS. To provide access to many users, an enterprise GIS stores data in commercial relational database management systems (RDBMSs), such as Oracle®, Informix® Dynamic Server, and Microsoft® SQL Server™, that have been spatially enabled by ESRI's ArcSDE™ (formerly SDE®) software.

Using ArcSDE allows GIS data to be viewed and edited by many people simultaneously. To make the most of a networked system's capabilities, multiple seats of key applications, such as ArcCatalog™, ArcMap™, and ArcToolbox™, are deployed on desktop machines across an organization. Servers supply them with data and perform processor-intensive tasks.

The functions of multiuser GIS are like those of project GIS, but on a larger scale and operating in a continuous, cyclical fashion. Planning is crucial for multiuser systems, but the rewards—including increased operational efficiency, better allocation of scarce resources, consistency of information, and better informed decisions—are tremendous.

Tasks you perform with ArcInfo

Whether you use ArcInfo in a project or multiuser environment, you can use the three desktop applications—ArcCatalog, ArcMap, and ArcToolbox—to do your work.

ArcCatalog

ArcCatalog lets you find, preview, document, and organize geographic data and create sophisticated geodatabases to store that data.

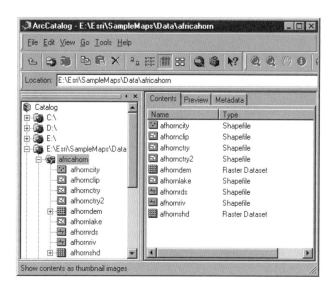

ArcCatalog provides a framework for organizing large and diverse stores of GIS data.

Different views of your data help you quickly find what you need, whether it is in a file, personal geodatabase, or remote RDBMS served by ArcSDE.

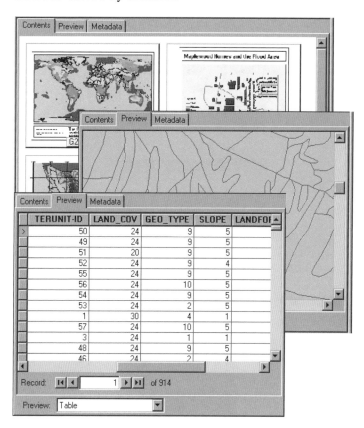

You can use ArcCatalog to organize folders and file-based data when you build project databases on your computer.

You can create personal geodatabases on your computer and use tools in ArcCatalog to create or import feature classes and tables.

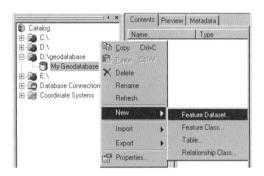

You can use wizards in ArcCatalog to define relationships within a geodatabase.

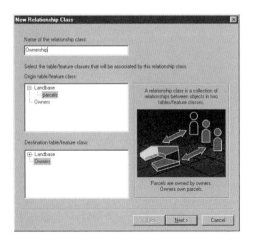

You can also design geodatabases with Computer-Aided Software Engineering (CASE) tools. These allow you to design custom objects and relationships in a geodatabase object model.

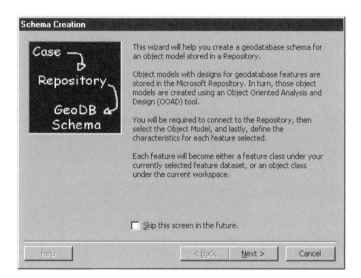

You can implement a geodatabase that you designed with a CASE tool, using ArcCatalog software's Schema Creation Wizard.

ArcMap

ArcMap lets you create and interact with maps. In ArcMap, you can view, edit, and analyze your geographic data.

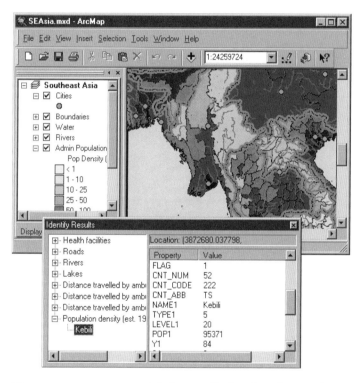

You can query your spatial data to find and understand relationships among geographic features.

You can symbolize your data in a wide variety of ways.

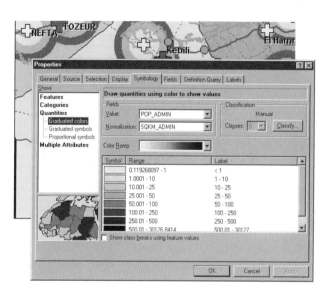

You can create charts and reports to communicate your understanding with others.

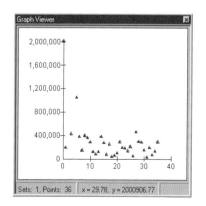

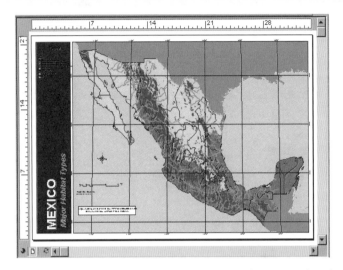

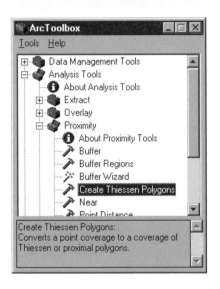

With ArcMap, you can create maps that integrate data in a wide variety of formats including shapefiles, coverages, tables, computer-aided drafting (CAD) drawings, images, grids, and triangulated irregular networks (TINs). You can lay out your maps in a what-you-see-is-what-you-get layout view.

ArcToolbox

ArcToolbox is a set of geoprocessing tools that give you the power of Workstation ArcInfo in a handy toolbox that can be rearranged to suit your work habits.

Simple geoprocessing tasks are accomplished through form-based tools.

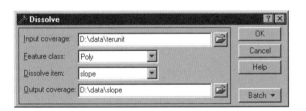

More complex operations can be done with the aid of wizards.

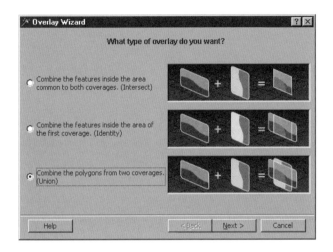

You can use tools to compose new ARC Macro Language (AML™) scripts and run existing AML scripts from ArcToolbox.

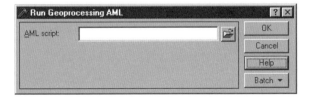

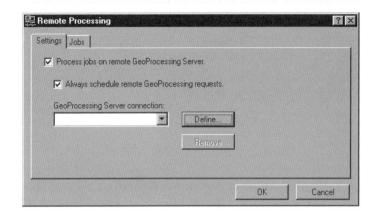

You can use your desktop computer to run your geoprocessing jobs, or you can designate a GeoProcessing Server on your network.

Designating a GeoProcessing Server lets you compose geoprocessing jobs on your desktop and run them at a scheduled time on a faster machine close to where the data is stored. This lets you leverage your organization's existing hardware, regardless of the platform (UNIX® or Windows NT®), and frees your desktop machine for other tasks.

Tips on learning ArcInfo

This book is intended to help you learn the basics of ArcInfo and GIS. You can also use the other books that come with ArcInfo to learn more.

When you want quick information about how to do a specific task, you can look it up in three handy reference books: *Using ArcCatalog*, *Using ArcMap*, and *Using ArcToolbox*. These books are organized around specific tasks. They provide answers in clear, concise steps with numbered graphics. Some of the chapters also contain background information if you want to find out more about the concepts behind a task.

If your job includes designing GIS databases or developing applications, or if you want to deepen your understanding of the organization of your GIS, you may want to read *Modeling Our World*. This book provides a broad conceptual discussion of GIS data models, with examples to illustrate the theory.

If you want task-oriented, step-by-step help creating a geodatabase, read *Building a Geodatabase*. This book will teach you how to take your geodatabase design and implement it in ArcInfo.

The *ArcObjects Developer's Guide* will introduce you to the development tools and environment that are available for customizing, extending, and creating extensions for ESRI end-user applications.

Exploring desktop ArcInfo

2

Maps are the most commonly used tools for understanding spatial information. Whether you do analysis or editing, produce wall maps or illustrate reports, design GIS databases or manage them—when you work with GIS you work with maps. ArcMap allows you to work with all of your geographic data in maps, regardless of the format or location of the underlying data. With ArcMap, you can assemble a map quickly from predefined layers, or you can add data from coverages, shapefiles, geodatabases, grids, images, and tables of coordinates or addresses.

Two other ArcInfo applications—ArcCatalog and ArcToolbox—are designed to work with ArcMap. You can browse, organize, and document your data holdings in ArcCatalog, send coverages from ArcCatalog to tools in ArcToolbox for sophisticated geoprocessing, and then drag and drop your results onto an existing map in ArcMap for display, analysis, and publication. It has never been easier to use the power of GIS.

In this chapter, you will create a map for a planning meeting of the Greenvalley City Council. You will use ArcCatalog to find the data and produce the map in ArcMap.

Introducing ArcCatalog

ArcCatalog is the tool for browsing, organizing, distributing, and documenting an organization's GIS data holdings.

In this exercise you work for the (fictitious) City of Greenvalley. The City Council is debating a proposal to build some more water mains downtown. As part of the process, the Council is reviewing water use in the downtown area.

You have been asked to make a map that shows the water mains in downtown Greenvalley and the relative water use at each parcel downtown.

To make the map easy to read, you will add the data to a general-purpose map of the town.

Start ArcCatalog

1. Click the Start button on the taskbar.

2. Point to Programs to display the Programs menu.

3. Point to ArcInfo.

4. Click ArcCatalog.

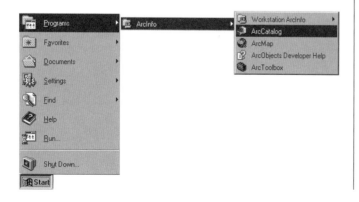

ArcCatalog starts and you see two panels in the ArcCatalog window.

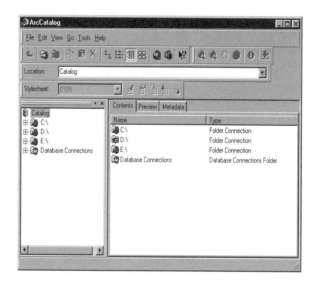

The *Catalog tree* on the left side of the ArcCatalog window is for browsing and organizing your GIS data. The contents of the current branch are displayed on the right side of the Catalog window.

Viewing data in ArcCatalog

When you need more information about a branch of the Catalog tree, you can use the Contents, Preview, and Metadata tabs to view your data in many different ways.

The ArcInfo coverage "cl" contains street centerlines. It is located on this computer's E:\ drive in a folder called City.

If you select a data source in the tree, you can view it in several ways, depending on the tab that you choose. Each tab has a toolbar associated with it that allows you to modify how you see your data.

These are Contents views:

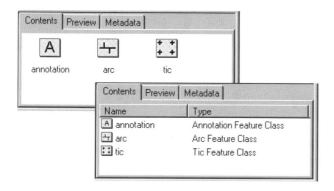

These are Preview views:

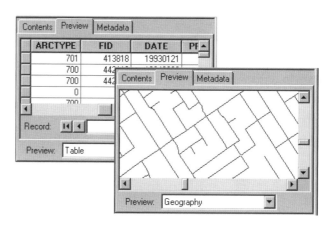

These are Metadata views:

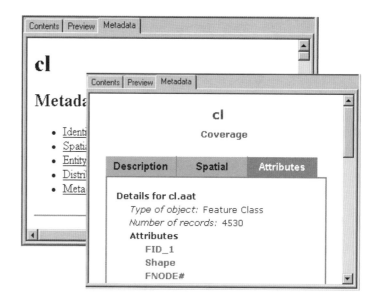

Connecting to your data

When you start ArcCatalog for the first time, the Catalog tree has a branch for each local hard drive, a branch for spatial reference files, and a branch for Database Connections. You can view the contents of a branch by double-clicking it or by clicking the plus sign beside it.

You can also create new branches in the Catalog tree to make it easier to navigate to your data. These branches are called *connections*.

You should check with your system administrator to find out where the tutorial data is installed on your system.

Make a connection to the tutorial data

Now you will add a connection to the folder that contains the tutorial data. This new branch in the Catalog tree will remain until you delete it.

1. Click the Connect to Folder button.

When you click the button a window opens that lets you browse to a folder on your computer or to a folder on another computer on your network.

2. Navigate to the ESRI\ArcTutor\Greenvalley folder on the drive where the tutorial data is installed. Click OK.

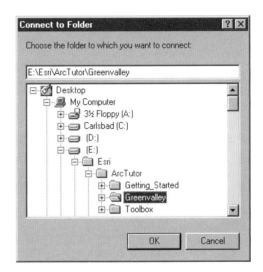

The new connection shows up as a branch in the Catalog tree.

Explore the Greenvalley folder connection

You can now look at the tutorial data that you have added.

1. Click the ESRI\ArcTutor\Greenvalley folder to view its contents on the right side of the ArcCatalog window.

2. Click the plus sign to expand the connection in the Catalog tree. This branch of the tree contains a folder, a map document, and a layer.

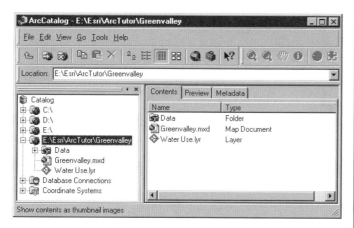

The Data folder has a special icon to show that it contains GIS data. You can customize ArcCatalog to recognize additional file types, for example text files, as GIS data.

The map, Greenvalley.mxd, is a general-purpose map of the City.

The Water Use layer shows a set of parcels in Greenvalley with a color scheme that indicates relative water use at each parcel.

Maps and layers

Maps and layers are important ways of organizing and displaying data in ArcInfo.

Maps, such as everyday paper maps, can contain many kinds of data. The data on a map is organized into layers, which are drawn on the map in a particular order. Each map contains a page layout where graphic elements such as legends, North arrows, scale bars, text, and other graphics are arranged. The layout shows the map page as it will be printed.

Layers define how a set of geographic features will be drawn when they are added to a map. They also act as shortcuts to the place where the data is actually stored— not necessarily the same place as where the layer file is stored. In this case, both the map and the layer refer to data that is stored in the Data folder.

If you store your geographic data in a central database, you can create maps and layers that refer to the database. This makes it easy to share maps and layers within an organization and eliminates the need to make duplicate copies of your data.

View the thumbnail sketch of the Greenvalley map

The right-hand panel in ArcCatalog displays a selected branch of the Catalog tree or dataset in many different ways. You can click an object in the tree view to view it in the right panel. One of the views that can be useful when you want to select a particular map is the thumbnail view.

1. Click the Thumbnails button on the Standard toolbar.

You can see the thumbnail sketch of the map. The other buttons on this toolbar let you view the contents of a folder in different ways.

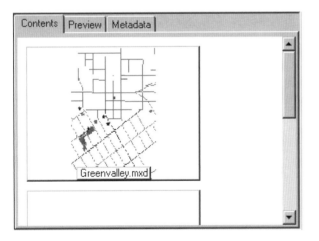

Open the Greenvalley map

You will use the Greenvalley map to provide context for the information that the City Council wants.

1. Double-click Greenvalley in the Catalog tree.

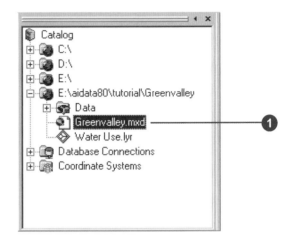

Double-clicking a map in the Catalog tree opens the map in ArcMap.

Sometimes you may want to start ArcMap without opening an existing map. You can start ArcMap by clicking the Launch ArcMap button in ArcCatalog.

Launch ArcMap button

You can also start ArcMap as you would any other program on your system, whether the Catalog tree is open or not.

Introducing ArcMap

ArcMap is the tool for creating, viewing, querying, editing, composing, and publishing maps.

Most maps present several types of information about an area at once. This map of Greenvalley contains three layers that show public buildings, streets, and parks.

You can see the layers in this map listed in the *table of contents*. Each layer has a check box that lets you turn it on or off.

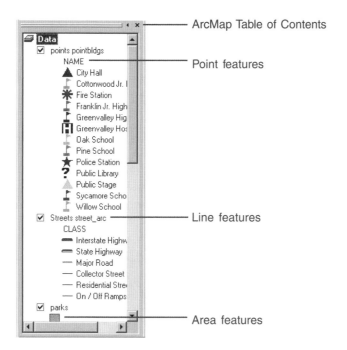

ArcMap Table of Contents

Point features

Line features

Area features

Within a layer, symbols are used to draw the *features*. In this case, buildings are represented by points, streets by

lines, and parks by areas. Each layer contains two kinds of information. The *spatial* information describes the location and shape of the geographic features. The *attribute* information tells you about other characteristics of the features.

In the park layer, all the features are drawn with a single green fill symbol. This single symbol lets you identify areas that are parks, but it does not tell you anything about the differences between the parks.

In the street layer, the features are drawn with different line symbols, according to the type of street that the lines represent. This symbol scheme lets you differentiate streets from other types of features and tells you something about the differences between the features as well.

In the buildings layer, the features are drawn with different point symbols. The shapes and colors of the symbols allow you to differentiate the institutions that they represent. All of the schools are grouped together and drawn with a particular symbol, so you can easily differentiate schools from the hospital or from City Hall. Each school symbol is drawn with a different color, which lets you differentiate Pine Elementary from Greenvalley High.

Working with maps

ArcInfo offers many ways to interact with maps.

Exploring

Maps let you see and interpret the spatial relationships among features. You could use the map you have just opened to find City Hall, to identify parks near schools, or to get the names of the streets around the library.

Analyzing

You can create new information and find hidden patterns by adding layers to a map. For example, if you added a layer of demographic information to the Greenvalley map you might use the resulting map to define school districts or find potential customers. If you added layers of geology and surface slope, you might use the map to identify areas at risk for landslides.

Presenting results

ArcMap makes it easy to lay out your maps for printing, embedding in other documents, or electronic publishing. You can quickly make great maps of your data. When you save a map, all of your layout work, symbols, text, and graphics are preserved.

ArcMap includes a vast array of tools for creating and using maps. In the rest of this chapter, you will use some of these tools.

Customizing

Maps are tools for getting a job done. You can create maps that have exactly the tools you need to help you complete your job quickly. You can easily customize the ArcMap interface by adding tools to existing toolbars (or removing them) or by creating custom toolbars. You can save these changes to the interface with a particular map or for every map that you open.

You can also use the Visual Basic® for Applications (VBA) programming language included in ArcMap to create new tools and interfaces. For example, you can create a VBA tool to make a table of the addresses of houses in a selected area. Once the tool is created, you can associate it with a custom toolbar and save it with a map for anyone to use.

Programming

You can build completely new interfaces for interacting with your maps and create new, specialized classes of features. ArcInfo 8 is built using Microsoft's Component Object Model (COM); all of the COM components are available to developers using a COM-compliant programming language. For more information about customizing ArcMap and ArcCatalog, refer to the *ArcObjects Developer's Guide*.

Exploring a map

You can explore a map in several ways. The Browse toolbar contains frequently used tools that let you navigate around the map, find features, and get information about them.

Zoom in and get information

If you want to see an area of the map in greater detail, you can zoom in to the map.

1. Click the Zoom In button.

2. Drag a box around one of the parks to zoom in to it.

   When you drag a box on the map after clicking the Zoom In button the map zooms to the new area. You can click the Back button to jump back to the previous map extent.

3. Click the Identify Features button and click the park.

   When you click a feature with the Identify Features tool, the Identify Results window appears. You can inspect the attributes of the feature from this window.

   If the tool finds several features where you clicked, it lists each feature on the left side of the window. You can click the features in this list to view their attributes on the right side of the window.

4. Close the Identify Results window.

Zoom to the map's full extent

If you have zoomed in to the map and want to see all of it, you can quickly zoom out to the map's full extent.

1. Click the Full Extent button.

Now you can see the full extent of the map. The map scale is around 1:95,000 (depending on your screen setup and the size of the ArcMap window), which you can see on the Standard toolbar.

At this scale, the building symbols are not visible. The Maximum Visible Scale *property* of this layer has been set to 1:70,000. You will change some of the properties of a layer later in this chapter.

Find a feature

The Find button lets you search a map for features that match your search criteria. The area you want to map is around the Greenvalley City Hall, so you will find City Hall and zoom to it.

1. Click the Find button.

When you click the Find button the Find dialog box appears. You can search for features from a particular layer or from all layers on the map.

2. Type "City Hall" in the Find text box. Click the In Layers dropdown arrow and click buildings_point. Click In fields, then click the dropdown arrow, and click Name. Click Find.

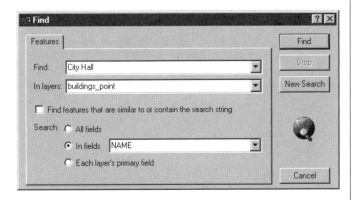

City Hall appears in the list of features that the tool has found.

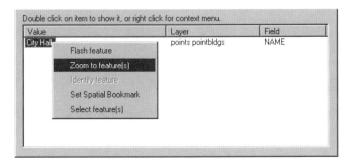

3. Right-click City Hall and click Zoom to feature(s).

   The map zooms to the City Hall. As the scale is now greater than the 1:70,000 threshold, the building features appear on the map and you can see the symbol for City Hall.

4. Click Cancel to close the Find dialog box.

The map now shows some of the area that you need to map for the City Council.

When you chose Zoom to feature(s), another option on the list was Set Spatial Bookmark. A *spatial bookmark* preserves a particular map extent so that you can zoom back to it whenever you want.

Spatial bookmarks are saved with a map, so anyone who opens a map can quickly zoom to a particular bookmarked area.

Zoom to a bookmarked area

Because you use this map to provide a context for other information, you have created some spatial bookmarks for the areas you frequently map. Downtown Greenvalley is one of these areas.

1. Click View and point to Bookmarks.

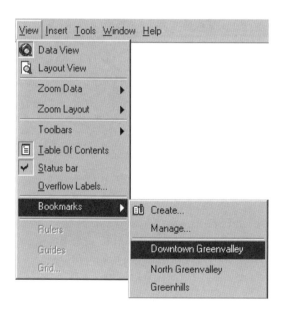

2. Click Downtown Greenvalley.

Now the map is zoomed to the downtown area. You have used this map extent and scale for previous maps of downtown Greenvalley. The map you are making will be easy for the Council members to compare with the other maps of the downtown area.

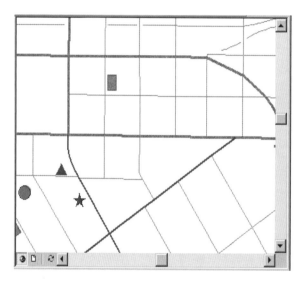

ArcMap provides an excellent interface for interactively exploring existing maps. You can use the tools you have just used and others to answer questions about particular features, find features, and view your maps at a variety of scales.

You can change the information that is displayed on maps by adding and removing layers and changing the way that layers are displayed.

In the next part of this chapter, you will add data to your map and change the properties of a layer.

Adding a layer to a map

Now that you have opened a map of Greenvalley and set the extent to downtown, it is time to make the map you need. The City Council wants the map to include downtown water use and the location and size of existing water mains. You will start by adding the Water Use layer to your map.

1. Position the ArcMap and ArcCatalog windows so that you can see both of them.

2. Click the Water Use layer in the Catalog and drag it onto the map. You can click and drag any layer from the Catalog tree onto an open map in ArcMap.

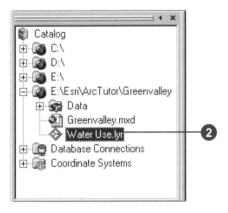

The layer shows parcels drawn with a graduated color ramp. Just as the roads and buildings were drawn with predetermined symbols when you opened the Greenvalley map, this layer is drawn with a particular set of symbols.

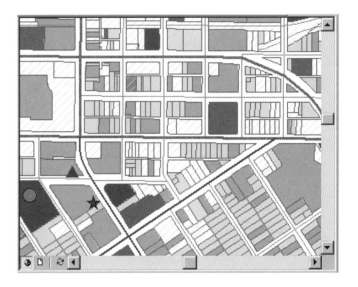

A layer serves as a shortcut to data. It also tells ArcMap how the data should be drawn. You can store layers in a place that is accessible to everyone in your organization who needs a particular set of data; the data will be displayed the same way for each of them.

As useful as layers are, sometimes they are not available. Fortunately, you can add raw geographic data to a map just as easily as you can add a layer.

Adding features from a database

When you add features directly from a coverage, shapefile, or database, they are all drawn with a single symbol.

Now you will add the water main features to your map.

1. Position the ArcMap and ArcCatalog windows so that you can see both of them.

2. Click the plus sign next to the Data folder in the Catalog tree to view the contents of the folder.

3. Click the plus sign next to GreenvalleyDB. GreenvalleyDB is a geodatabase that contains the data you are using. The data in this geodatabase is organized in four feature datasets: Public Buildings, Parks, Public Utility, and Transportation.

4. Click the plus sign next to Public Utility.

5. Click watermains_arc and drag it onto your map.

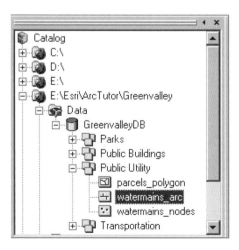

Watermains_arc is a feature class—a collection of features represented with the same geometry (shape). In this case, the features are polyline shapes that represent the pipes in the water distribution system; they were drawn on the map with green line symbols.

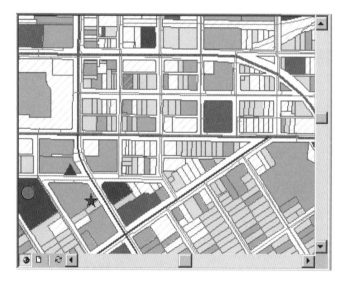

When you add a new feature class to a map, it is placed in the table of contents with features of the same geometry, so watermains_arc appears in the table of contents above streets_arc.

Geodatabases containing feature datasets and feature classes are a new way ArcInfo manages geographic information. In Chapter 3, you will learn more about these and other GIS data types.

Changing the way features are drawn

The Council wants to know the approximate sizes of the water mains downtown, so you must assign some new symbols to the features.

1. Right-click watermains_arc in the ArcMap table of contents and click Properties.

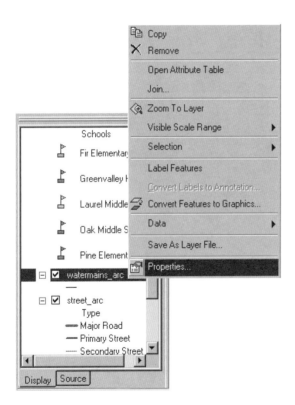

The Layer Properties dialog box appears. You can use this dialog box to inspect and change a wide variety of layer properties.

The water mains feature class includes several attributes of the water mains. As the Council wants to know the sizes of the water mains, you will group the mains into five classes based on their diameter attribute.

2. Click the Symbology tab on the Properties dialog box.

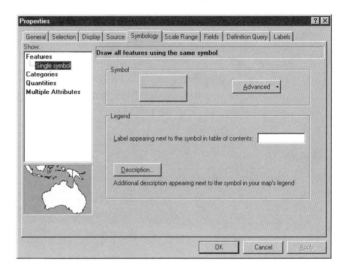

You can change the symbol scheme for the layer, as well as its appearance in the table of contents, from this tab.

3. Click Quantities. The panel changes to give you controls for drawing with graduated colors.

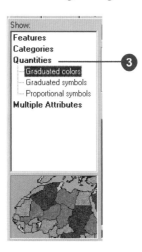

4. Click Graduated symbols. The panel changes to give you controls for drawing with graduated symbols.

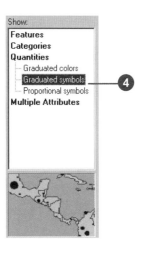

5. Click the Value dropdown arrow and click Diameter. ArcMap assigns the data to five classes using the Natural Breaks classification (Jenks' method).

Now the width of the line symbols indicates the diameter of the water mains. You want the water mains to be blue, so you will change the base symbol.

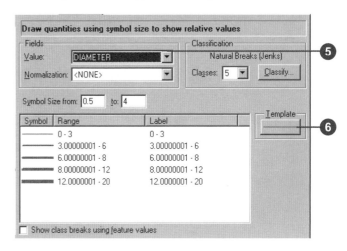

6. Click Template.

When you click Template the Symbol Selector dialog box appears. Here you can choose predefined symbols, such as the Highway line symbol, or you can design your own symbols.

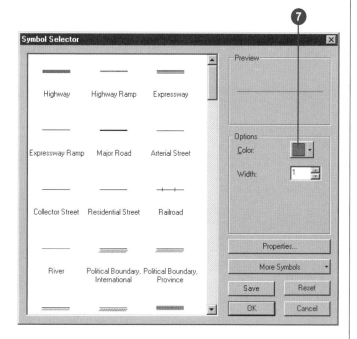

7. Click Color. The color selector dialog appears. You can select one of the predefined colors from this palette or click More Colors to mix your own colors using one of several popular color models.

8. Choose a dark shade of blue and click OK.

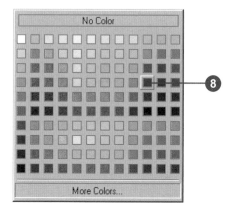

Now all of the water mains will be drawn with dark blue lines, with the line width representing the diameter of the water main.

9. Click OK on the Properties dialog box to see your map with the new line symbols.

As you have seen, ArcMap has a rich set of line symbol selection and editing tools. These and other tools also work with point and polygon symbols.

Once you have set the symbolization for a layer to your satisfaction, you can preserve it for later use by saving the map or by saving the layer as its own layer file such as the Water Use layer you added.

Adding labels to a map

The map now shows some of the street centerlines and water mains with similar symbols. To avoid confusing a map reader, you will add street names on the map and change the street centerline symbol.

1. Right-click street_arc in the table of contents.

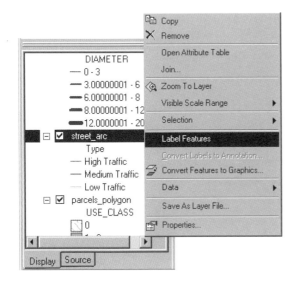

2. Click Label Features.

   ArcMap adds the names of the streets to the map.

Change the street centerline symbol

1. Right-click street_arc in the table of contents again and click Properties.

2. Click the Symbology tab.

3. Click Features.

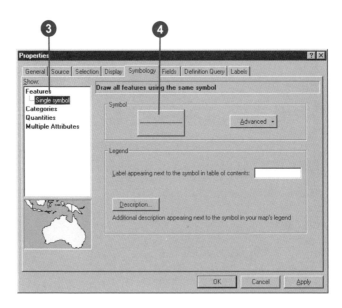

The street centerlines will now be drawn with a single symbol. You will change the default line color to a light gray, so the centerlines will be visible but unobtrusive.

4. Click the line symbol.

The Symbol Selector appears.

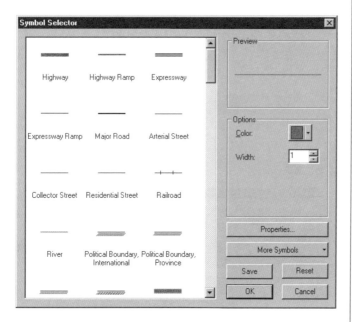

5. Click Color. Click a light gray and Click OK.

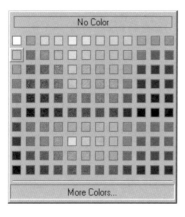

6. Click OK on the Properties dialog box.

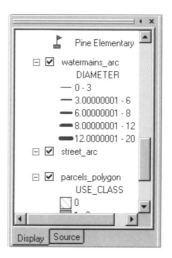

Now the centerlines will be drawn in a light gray, so they will not be confused with the water mains.

Working with the map layout

All of the data you need is now on the map and has symbols. The map that you are making for the Council meeting will be printed in color on an 8.5" x 11" sheet of paper and distributed to each council member.

1. Click View and click Layout View.

Now you can see the map on a virtual page. The layers of data appear in a *data frame* on the page. Data frames are a way of organizing the layers you want to see together on a map.

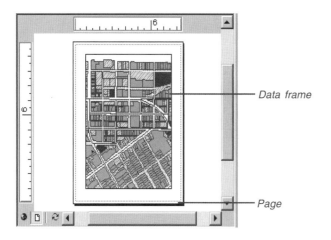

Data frame

Page

There is always at least one data frame on a map. This one is called Layers; you can see its name at the top of the ArcMap table of contents.

You can add additional data frames to a map to compare two areas side by side or to show overviews or detailed insets.

You can see all of the data frames on your map in Layout view. If you switch back to Data view, you will see the layers that are in the active data frame. The active data frame is shown in boldface type in the table of contents.

In Layout view you can change the shape and position of the data frame on the page, add other map elements such as scale bars and legends to the map, and change the page size and orientation.

The Layout toolbar is added to the ArcMap interface when you choose Layout View.

You can use the tools on the Layout toolbar to change the size and position of the virtual page on your screen or to zoom in or out of the virtual page.

You can also use tools from the Tools toolbar in Layout View to change the extent of the layers that are shown in the data frame.

2. Right-click on the page and choose Page Setup.

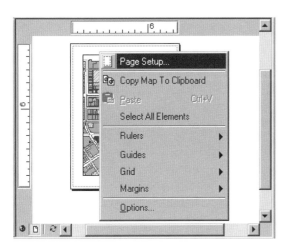

3. Click Landscape to change the page orientation and then click OK.

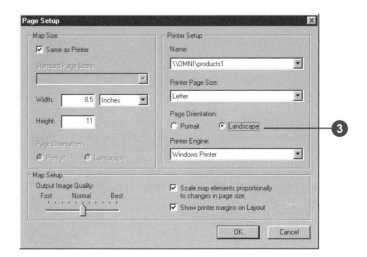

Now the page is in landscape orientation.

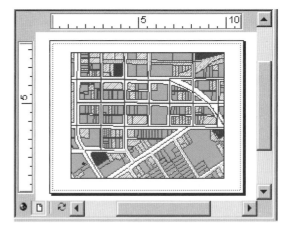

You will add a scale bar, North arrow, legend, and title to the page to help the Council members use the map.

First, you will make some space on the page for these other map elements.

4. Click the Select Graphics button.

5. Click the data frame to select it. The data frame is now outlined with a dashed line and has selection handles at its corners and edges.

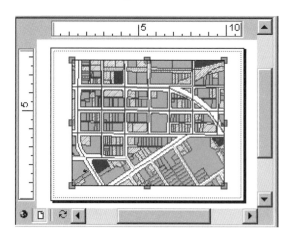

6. Point to the selection handle at the lower-right corner of the data frame. The cursor becomes a two-pointed resize cursor. Click the corner and drag it up and to the left.

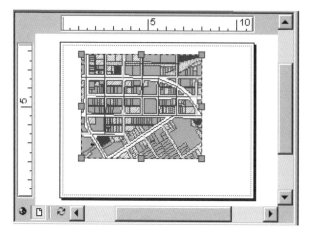

Add a scale bar

1. From the Insert menu choose Scale Bar.

The Scalebar Selector dialog appears.

2. Click one of the scale bars and click OK.

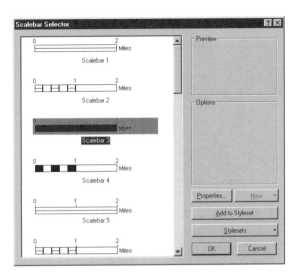

3. Click the scale bar and drag it to the empty space below the left side of the data frame.

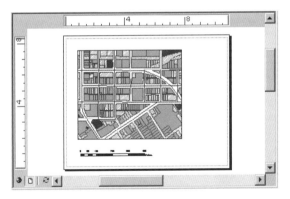

Add a North arrow

1. Click Insert and click North Arrow.

The North Arrow Selector appears.

2. Click one of the North arrows and click OK.

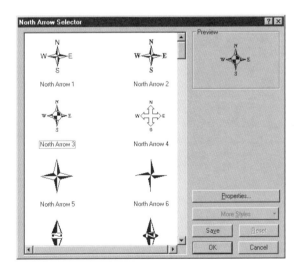

3. Click the North arrow and drag it to the empty space below the data frame and to the right of the scale bar.

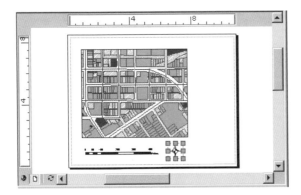

Add a legend

1. Click Insert and click Legend.

2. Click the legend and drag it to the empty space to the right of the data frame.

You can click the blue selection handles to resize the legend so that it fits along the right side of the page.

Add a title

1. Click Insert and click Title.

The title "Greenvalley" appears on the map.

Greenvalley is the name of the map document, but you will need a more explanatory title on the map.

2. Type "Downtown Greenvalley Water Mains and Water Use". Press Enter. ArcMap centers the title on the page.

Saving a map

You have made a lot of changes to this map. Because you want to keep the new map that you have created and also keep the old template map, you will use Save As to save this map under a new name.

1. Click File and click Save As.

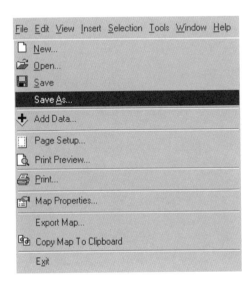

2. Navigate to the \Esri\ArcTutor\Greenvalley folder.

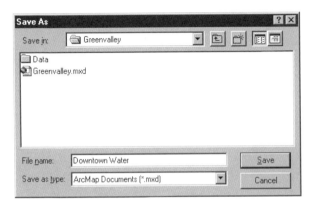

3. Type "Downtown Water". Click Save.

Now you are ready to print a copy of this map for the City Council.

Printing a map

You can easily print the maps you have composed in ArcMap. The Layout view lets you arrange map elements, such as data frames, scale bars, and North arrows, on the page exactly as you want them to print.

You can print your maps using any printer on your network, and you can choose to print using Windows®, PostScript®, or ArcPress™ (if installed) printer engines.

1. Click File and click Print.

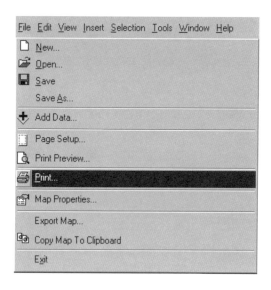

The Print dialog box appears. You can change the default printer by clicking Setup.

2. Click OK.

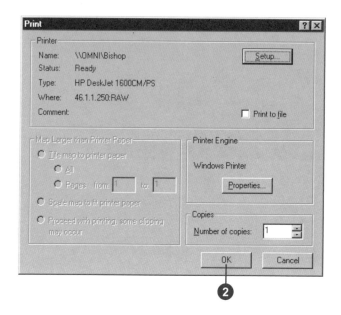

You are ready to take the map to the Council meeting.

What's next?

While making your first map in ArcInfo 8, you have learned how to start and use two Desktop ArcInfo applications: ArcCatalog and ArcMap.

In the next chapter you will learn more about GIS data and how to work with various data types in ArcInfo.

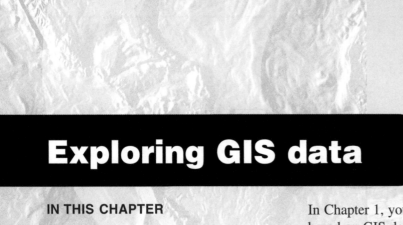

Exploring GIS data

In Chapter 1, you worked with a map and layers. The layers on a map are based on GIS data. When you added the water mains to the map, you added data from a feature class stored in a geodatabase. Other formats for GIS data include shapefiles, coverages, and images. GIS data formats vary, but they all store spatial and attribute information.

Much data has a spatial component that is not widely recognized. For example, customer databases often include addresses. With a suitable street dataset, these addresses can be plotted as points or geocoded. Similarly, tables of sales figures can be linked by a query statement to a feature class of sales territories and displayed on a map.

It is useful to understand the different GIS data types and database models when you are conducting an analysis project. This chapter contains a brief discussion of common types of GIS data and database models.

Geographic data models

ArcInfo stores and manages geographic data in a number of formats. Some of the different formats reflect different models of the world, while others reflect different implementations of the same model of the world. The three basic models of the world that ArcInfo uses are vector, raster, and TIN.

Vector models

Many aspects of the world can be represented with points, lines, and areas. This kind of representation is generically called a *vector* model of the world. Vector models of the world are particularly useful for representing and storing discrete features such as buildings, pipes, or parcel boundaries.

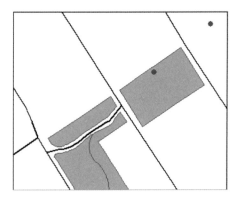

Points, lines, and areas are stored as coordinates or sets of connected coordinates that define a shape.

ArcInfo stores vector data as features in feature classes and collections of feature classes. You can choose from three implementations of the vector model to represent your feature data: coverages, shapefiles, and geodatabases. These are discussed in detail later in this chapter.

Raster models

In a *raster* model, the world is represented as a surface that is divided into a regular grid of cells. Raster models are useful for storing data that varies continuously. Each cell contains a value that can represent membership in a class, a measurement, or an interpreted value. An aerial photograph, a satellite image, a surface of chemical concentrations, and an elevation surface are examples of geographic information suited to a raster model.

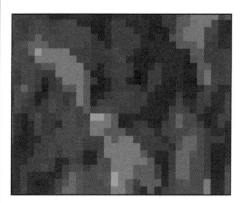

The smaller the cell size, the higher the resolution and the more detailed the map. However, because the cells form a regular grid over the whole surface, decreasing the cell size to store higher resolution data substantially increases the total volume of data that must be stored.

ArcInfo stores all kinds of raster data as raster datasets in geodatabases. ArcInfo can recognize and use rasters from image files in many different file types and from grids stored in coverage workspaces. Please see the online documentation for more information about raster data.

TIN models

In a *triangulated irregular network* model, the world is represented as a network of linked triangles drawn between irregularly spaced points with x, y, and z values. TINs are an efficient way to store and analyze surfaces.

Heterogeneous surfaces that vary sharply in some areas and less in others can be modeled more accurately in a given volume of data with a triangulated surface than with a raster. That is because many points can be placed where

the surface is highly variable and fewer points can be placed where the surface is less variable. ArcInfo stores triangulated surfaces as TIN datasets. Please see the online documentation for more information about TINs.

Working with grids, images, and TINs

You can add grid, image, and TIN datasets to a map just as you would features, and you can inspect and organize them with ArcCatalog.

ArcToolbox contains tools for performing some basic operations on grid and TIN datasets such as cut-and-fill, volume, and visibility analyses. It also contains conversion tools for converting between the formats, deriving contour lines from them, and importing surfaces to grids or TINs from other formats.

For more information about GIS data models, please see the online documentation or the book *Modeling Our World.*

Tabular data

You can think of a GIS as a database that understands geometry. Like other databases, ArcInfo lets you link tables of data together. Just about any table of data can be joined to an existing feature class if they share an attribute.

Geolocating is another means of getting tabular data on a map. Perhaps the simplest example of geolocating is plotting points based on tables of x,y coordinates. You can also plot points by geolocating tables of addresses on an existing street network. This is often called geocoding addresses.

Formats of feature data

ArcInfo uses three main formats of feature data: coverages, shapefiles, and geodatabases. Each represents the world with a different vector model, but ArcMap and ArcCatalog treat feature data in all three formats as feature classes.

Coverages and shapefiles employ a *georelational data model*. They store the vector data for the features in binary files and use unique identifiers to link features to attributes stored in feature attribute tables in other files.

Geodatabases employ a *geodatabase data model*. In this model, features are stored as rows in a relational database table.

Coverages

Coverages are the standard format for complex geoprocessing, building high-quality geographic datasets, and sophisticated spatial analysis. Coverages are the best choice if your work requires the routes and sections used in linear measurement systems (dynamic segmentation) as these are not supported by geodatabases at the present time.

Coverages contain primary, composite, and secondary feature types. The *primary* features in coverages are label points, arcs, and polygons. The *composite* features, routes/sections and regions are built from these primary feature types.

Coverages may also contain *secondary* features: tics, links, and annotation. Tics and links do not represent geographic objects but are used to manage coverages. Annotation is used to provide text about geographic features on maps.

Primary features in coverages

Label points can represent individual point features, for example, wells. In the diagram below, the point on the left represents well number 57. Label points also link attributes to polygons. Each polygon in a coverage has a single label point with its feature ID number, usually located near the polygon's center. The diagram on the right shows the label points of polygons 102 and 103.

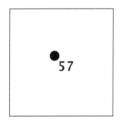 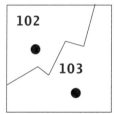

Arcs are connected sets of line segments, with nodes at the endpoints. A single arc can stand alone such as a fault line on a geologic map; many arcs can be organized into line networks such as stream or utility networks; or they can be organized into polygons that represent areas such as soil types.

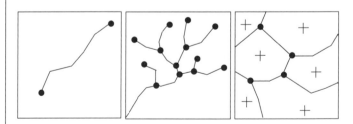

Nodes are the endpoints of and connections between arcs. Nodes can have attributes, so they can represent point features in a network such as valves in a network of water mains.

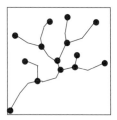

Nodes are important for tracking how features in coverages are connected to each other; this is called *topology*. You will learn more about topology in the 'What is coverage topology?' section of Chapter 6.

Polygons represent areas. They are bounded by arcs including arcs that define island polygons. Polygons in a coverage may share arcs such as B and C below, but they do not overlap. Each point in an area falls within exactly one polygon, so for example, a point within polygon A is outside of polygon B.

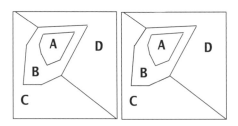

Composite features in coverages

Routes and *sections* are linear features that are composed of arcs and parts of arcs. Routes define paths along an existing linear network such as the route from a house to an airport along a street network.

Because points of interest on a network are not always at nodes, sections identify partial arcs. They record how far along a given arc a route begins or ends.

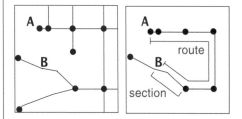

Regions are area features that are composed of polygons. Unlike polygons, regions can be discontinuous. For example, the mainland and an island can be mapped as two polygons, but they can belong to the same region.

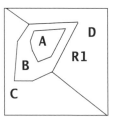

In the diagram above, polygons A and D belong to region 1.

Regions in a coverage can also overlap. For example, in a coverage of forest polygons, two regions that represent different forest fires could overlap if an area that burned in one year also burned in another.

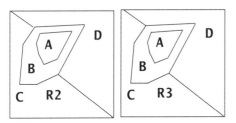

In the diagram above, region 2 and region 3 share polygon C.

Secondary features in coverages

Annotation features are text strings that describe a feature when a map is displayed or printed. Annotation can be positioned at a point, between two points, or along a series of points. Annotation is used to make maps easier to read and understand.

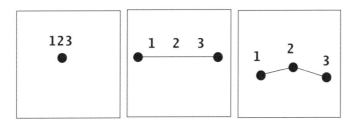

Tics are geographic control points. They represent known locations on the ground and are used to register and transform the coordinates of a coverage.

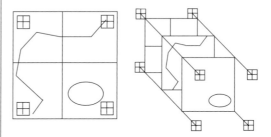

Tics allow features digitized from a paper map to be accurately transformed from digitizer units such as centimeters or inches to real-world units such as kilometers or miles. It is a good practice to use the same tic locations when you digitize sets of features from a map into different coverages, so they will overlay correctly.

Links are displacement vectors that are used to adjust the shape of coverages, for example to match the edges of adjacent coverages. Links consist of a from-point and a to-point.

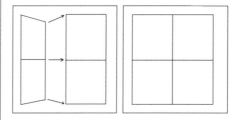

Storage of coverages

Coverages are stored in workspaces. A workspace is a folder in the file system. The workspace folder contains a folder named info and folders named for each coverage in the workspace.

Here, the workspace is called a_workspace, and the coverages are called a_coverage and b_coverage.

Workspace in the file system

A coverage folder contains a set of files that store information about the features in the coverage. The attributes of coverage features are stored in feature attribute tables that are managed by an INFO™ database. The info folder contains INFO data files and table definitions for each coverage.

In ArcCatalog, you see a coverage workspace as a GIS data folder. You can identify the geometry of a coverage by

Workspace in ArcCatalog

its icon. You can also see the feature classes within a coverage.

Here, you can see that a_workspace contains two coverages: a_coverage and b_coverage. The a_coverage contains an arc feature class and a tic feature class. This coverage has polygon topology, so it contains a polygon feature class and a label feature class as well. The dataset b_coverage is a line coverage, so it just contains arc and tic feature classes.

You may also see additional data tables in a coverage workspace if there are other tables stored in the INFO database.

Special tools for coverages

All of the power of the ArcInfo command line interface, including AML, is available for use with coverages. ArcToolbox provides convenient, Windows-based tools and wizards for working with coverages.

The tools in ArcToolbox help you perform a wide variety of operations on coverages. For example, the Build and Clean tools are used to create and maintain line and polygon topology for coverages. The Overlay wizard helps you perform a variety of overlay operations. Other tools in ArcToolbox can be used to convert data between many different formats including the geodatabase format.

You can manage your coverages with ArcCatalog and make maps with them using ArcMap.

Shapefiles

Shapefiles are useful for mapmaking and some kinds of analysis. A great deal of geographic data is available in the shapefile format.

Shapefiles are a nontopological vector data format. Shapefiles are simpler than coverages because they do not store topological associations among different features and feature classes. Each shapefile stores features belonging to a single feature class.

Features in shapefiles

Shapefiles have two types of point features: points and multipoints. They have line features that can be simple lines or multipart polylines. They also have area features that are simple or multipart areas called polygons.

Point shapes are simply single-point features such as wells or monuments. They are not associated with polygons. Here, well number 57 is selected.

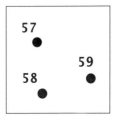

Multipoint shapes are collections of points that all represent one feature. A group of small islands could be represented as a single multipoint shape. Here, multipoint feature 22 is selected.

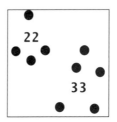

Line shapes can be simple continuous lines such as a fault line on a map. They can also be polylines that branch such as a river. Line shapes can also have discontinuous parts.

There are no topological relationships between lines in a shapefile. Line shapes are not associated with points or polygons.

Polygon shapes can be simple areas such as a single island. They can also be multipart areas such as several islands that constitute a single state.

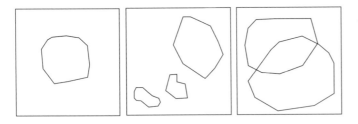

Polygon shapes can overlap, but the shapefile does not store topological relationships between them. The market areas of two stores could be represented as overlapping polygon shapes. Polygon shapes are not associated with lines or points.

Special tools for shapefiles

You can use ArcMap software's editing tools on shapefiles and on geodatabase feature classes. ArcToolbox and ArcCatalog contain tools that let you convert feature data between the shapefile and coverage formats and the shapefile and geodatabase formats.

Storage of shapefiles

Shapefiles are stored in folders. A shapefile consists of a set of files of vector data in the shapefile and a dBASE®

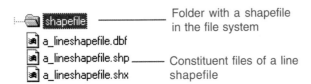

Folder with a shapefile in the file system

Constituent files of a line shapefile

.dbf file of the attributes of the shapes. Each constituent file shares the shapefile name.

A shapefile contains shapes of only one geometry: point, multipoint, line, or polygon. When you look at a folder of shapefiles in ArcCatalog, you see the shapefiles as standalone feature classes.

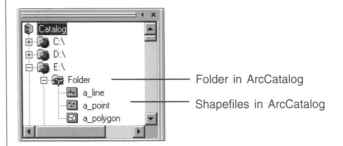

Folder in ArcCatalog

Shapefiles in ArcCatalog

Geodatabases

Geodatabases implement an object-oriented GIS data model, the geodatabase data model.

Some advantages of this model are features in geodatabases can have built-in behavior, geodatabase features are completely stored in a single database, and large geodatabase feature classes can be stored seamlessly, not tiled.

In addition to generic features such as points, lines, and areas, you can create custom features such as transformers, pipes, and parcels. Custom features can have special behavior to better represent real-world objects. You can use this behavior to support sophisticated modeling of networks, data entry error prevention, custom rendering of features, and custom forms for inspecting or entering attributes of features.

Features in geodatabases

Because you can create your own custom objects, the number of potential feature classes is unlimited. The basic geometries (shapes) for geodatabase feature classes are points, multipoints, network junctions, lines, network edges, and polygons. You can also create features with new geometries.

Point and *multipoint* geodatabase features are similar to the corresponding feature types in shapefiles.

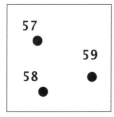
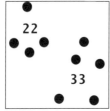

Generic point features could represent building locations in a city, as they did in the Greenvalley tutorial example.

Custom point features could also represent buildings, but they might include an interface that would list the owner, area, and assessed value of the building or display a photograph or schematic of the building.

Network junction features are points that play a topological role in a network, somewhat like nodes in a coverage. There are simple and complex network junction features.

A *simple junction feature* might be used to represent a fitting that connects two pipes. It could have validation behavior that would ensure that it connected pipes of the correct diameter and materials.

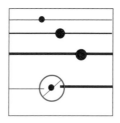

A *complex junction feature* plays a more complex role in a network. It can contain internal parts that play a logical and topological role in the larger network.

For example, a complex junction feature could be used to represent a switch in an electric power network. In one position the switch could connect point A to point B, while in another position it could connect point A to point C.

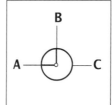

The switch might have editing validation rules that would control the types of power lines that could be connected to it. It could have custom behavior that would draw it with different symbols depending on its state.

Line features are lines built from three kinds of segments: line segments, circular arcs, and Bezier splines. A single line could be built from all three parts, as in the illustration on the right, below.

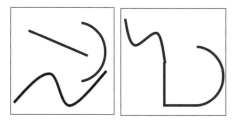

Lines can be used to represent linear geographic features such as roads or contour lines. Line features can have custom drawing behavior that generalizes the line depending on the map scale or that controls the placement of annotation along the line.

Network edge features are lines that play a topological role in a network. They can be used for tracing and analysis. Here, the network between A and B has been traced. The network contains simple and complex network edge features.

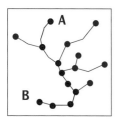

A *simple edge feature* is a linear network feature that connects to junction features at its endpoints. In this respect simple edge features are similar to arcs, which have nodes at their endpoints. A simple edge feature could be used to represent a pipe in a water network.

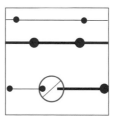

Simple edge features can have connectivity rules; for instance, a 10-cm pipe must connect to a 10-cm fitting. They can also have special class methods, so a pipe feature could calculate the pressure drop of a liquid flowing from one end to another, based on the pipe diameter, roughness, and length. They can have special query, editing, and data entry interfaces.

A *complex edge feature* is a linear network feature that can support one or more junctions along its length, yet remain a single feature. In the example below, the line from A to B is a single complex edge feature.

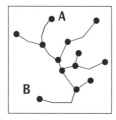

A power line could be represented as a single complex edge feature. It could have junction features at its ends and additional junctions where other lines attach to it along its length. Similar to simple edge features, complex edge features can have special class methods and interfaces.

Polygon features represent areas. Their boundaries can be composed of line, circular arc, and Bezier spline segments. They can be simple closed shapes or they can have discontinuous parts. Polygon features can also have nested islands and lakes.

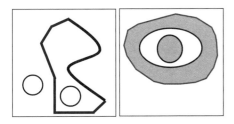

You can use polygon features to represent geographic features such as buildings, census blocks, or forest stands. Polygon features, such as other geodatabase features, can have customized behavior and interfaces. A custom building polygon could be drawn as a plan view at one scale, as a generalized building footprint at another, and with a point symbol at another. It could also have a custom interface for editing and viewing its attributes.

Special tools for geodatabases

ArcMap lets you view and edit geodatabase features. ArcCatalog lets you create and manage geodatabases and the feature classes and feature datasets within them. Wizards and tools in ArcToolbox and ArcCatalog make it easy to convert existing feature data from shapefiles or coverages into geodatabase feature classes.

You can use the ArcToolbox Geometric Network Wizard to build geometric networks from multiple feature classes contained in the same feature dataset.

You can create your own custom geodatabases from scratch, or you can modify elements of an existing geodatabase. For more information about designing geodatabases and creating custom features, see the books *Modeling Our World* and *Building a Geodatabase*.

Storage of geodatabase features

Geodatabase features reside in geodatabases. A multiuser, versioned geodatabase can be implemented using ArcSDE software in any of the leading commercial all-relational databases. Single-user geodatabases can be implemented in a Microsoft .mdb file.

A geodatabase stores each feature as a row in a table. The table is a feature class. The vector shape of the feature is stored in the table's shape field. Geodatabases can also store data tables and references to other tables.

Geodatabase feature classes each contain one geometric feature type. Related feature classes can be organized into feature datasets. Topologically related edge and junction features within a dataset can be bound into a geometric network.

Geodatabase feature classes are stored with spatial indexes, so you can work efficiently with small areas of very large seamless databases. This eliminates the need to divide large, complex datasets into separate tiles.

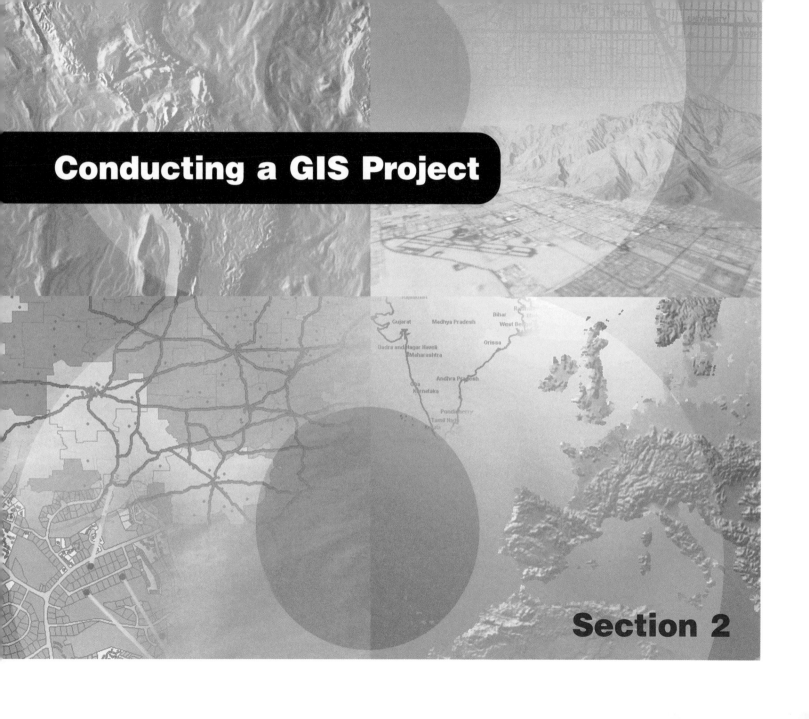

Conducting a GIS Project

Section 2

Planning a GIS project

4

Beginning with this chapter and through the rest of the book, you will conduct a GIS project. The tasks you perform will help you learn the methods for performing your own GIS projects. The scenario for the project involves finding the best site for a new wastewater recycling plant for the small City of Greenvalley. This chapter will introduce this scenario, provide a conceptual overview of what GIS analysis is all about, and present the steps involved in conducting a GIS project.

In this chapter you will prepare to conduct a GIS analysis to find a suitable site for the new plant. You will learn about several specific GIS analysis techniques and, perhaps more importantly, you will learn how to plan and carry out a GIS analysis project.

To find a suitable site you will need to know the site selection critera, identify data needed to match these criteria, and use the data to find suitable sites. These are fundamental elements of a GIS analysis.

What is a GIS analysis?

The phrase "GIS analysis" encompases a wide variety of operations that you can do with a geographic information system. These range from simple display of features to complex, multistep analytical models.

Showing the geographic distribution of data

Perhaps the simplest form of GIS analysis is presenting the geographic distribution of data. This is conceptually the same as sticking pins in a wall map, a simple but powerful method of detecting patterns.

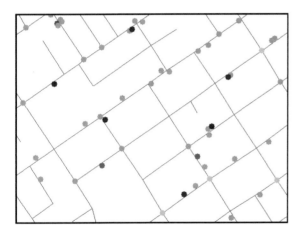

Here, the map is the analysis. A police department might analyze burglary patterns by plotting the addresses of reported break-ins. The department could make the map more informative by displaying the incidents with different symbols to show the time of day, method of entry, or types of valuables reported stolen.

Querying GIS data

Another type of GIS analysis is querying, or selecting from, the database. Queries let you identify and focus on a specific set of features. There are two types of GIS queries, *attribute* and *location* queries. Attribute queries, also called aspatial queries, find features based upon their attributes.

The police department mentioned above could use an attribute query of their database to obtain a table of crimes that fall into a particular category.

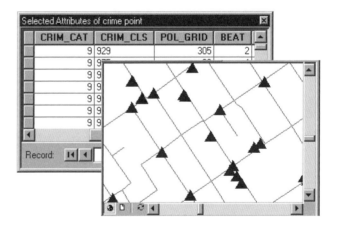

Here are the results from a query on the crime_cat field, showing records where the value in the field is 9. The map shows the results of the query.

Location queries, also called spatial queries, find features based on where they are. The police department could use a location query of the database to find crimes that occurred within a given area.

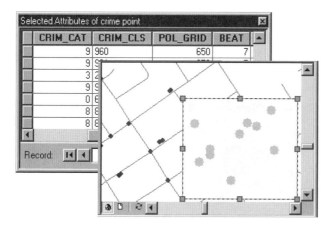

One way to do a location query is by drawing a rectangle on the map. Here, the police department has selected only those crimes that occurred within the rectangle. These crimes could be studied together to determine if any of them are related.

The police department could also do more complex spatial queries using polygon features, such as census tracts, selected from another layer. One of the most useful features of a GIS is that you can see the results of both spatial and aspatial queries on the map.

Identifying what is nearby

A third type of GIS analysis is finding what is near a feature. One way to find what is near a feature is by creating a buffer around the feature.

A city planning commission could identify areas within 1,000 meters of a proposed airport by buffering the airport feature. The buffer could be used with other layers of data to show which schools or hospitals would be near the new airport.

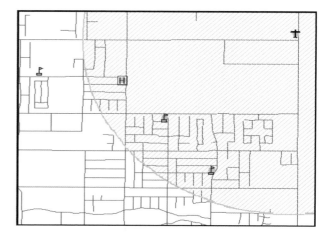

A powerful function of GIS analysis is that the output of one procedure can be used in another. Here, the buffer around the airport is used in a location query. Two schools and a hospital that are within the buffer have been selected. The school that is outside of the buffer was not selected.

Overlaying different layers

A fourth type of GIS analysis is overlaying different layers of features. You can create new information when you overlay one set of features with another. There are several types of overlay operations, but all involve joining two existing sets of features into a single new set of features.

For example, a farmer wants to find how much land can be planted with a new crop. The crop can't be planted on hillsides and needs soils that are highly permeable.

The farmer combines two existing layers of data about the farm: polygons of the ground surface classified by slope and polygons of soil permeability in a *union* overlay. The farmer can now select the new polygons that have low slopes and high permeability.

Low slope   High permeability   Low slope and high permeability

There are several different spatial overlay and spatial manipulation operations that you can use on features in coverages. These are available as tools in ArcToolbox and from the Overlay wizard in ArcToolbox. Because these tools require topology, they can only be used on coverages. You can use some tools in the ArcMap Editor to do some similar overlay operations with shapefile and geodatabase features.

Doing a complex analysis

You can combine all of these techniques and many others in a complex GIS analysis. With a GIS you can create detailed models of the world to solve complicated problems. Because a GIS can perform these operations rapidly, it is possible to repeat an analysis using slightly different parameters each time and compare the results. This can allow you to refine your analysis techniques.

Next you will learn about the steps in a typical GIS analysis.

The steps in a GIS project

When you conduct a GIS analysis, you must identify the objectives of the project, create a project database containing the data you need to solve the problem, use GIS functions to create an analytical model to solve the problem, and present the results.

Step 1: Identify your objectives

The first step of the process is to identify the objective of the analysis. You should consider the following questions when you are identifying your objectives:

- What is the problem to solve? How is it solved now? Are there alternate ways to solve it using a GIS?

- What are the final products of the project—reports, working maps, presentation-quality maps?

- Who is the intended audience of these products—the public, technicians, planners, officials?

- Will the data be used for other purposes? What are the requirements for these other purposes?

This step is important because the answers to these questions determine the scope of the project as well as how you go about implementing the analysis.

Step 2: Create a project database

The second step is to create a project database. The project database may include data in different formats, depending on the operations that you will use. Topological overlay functions require coverage data, but selection by layer and queries can be done on shapefiles and geodatabase feature classes.

Creating the project database is a three-step process. The steps are designing the database, automating and gathering data for the database, and managing the database.

Designing the database includes identifying the spatial data you will need, determining the required feature attributes, setting the study area boundary, choosing the coordinate system to use, and choosing the attributes each feature type needs.

Automating the data involves digitizing or converting data from other systems and formats into a usable format as well as verifying the data, correcting errors, and creating topology.

Managing the database involves putting spatial data into the same real-world coordinate system and joining adjacent coverages.

Creating the project database is a critical and time-consuming part of the project. The completeness and accuracy of the data you use in your analysis determines the accuracy of the final products.

Step 3: Analyze the data

The third step is to analyze the data. Analyzing data in a GIS is often referred to as spatial modeling. A model is a representation of reality used to simulate a process, predict an outcome, or analyze a problem.

A spatial model involves applying one or more of three categories of GIS function to some spatial data. These functions are

Geometric modeling functions—calculating distances, generating buffers, and calculating areas and perimeters

Coincidence modeling functions—overlay of datasets to find places where values coincide

Adjacency modeling functions—allocating, pathfinding, and redistricting

With a GIS you can quickly perform analyses that would be impossible or extremely time consuming if done by hand. You create alternative scenarios by changing your methods or parameters and running the analysis again.

Step 4: Present the results

The fourth step is to present the results of your analysis. Your final product should effectively communicate your findings to your audience. Often the results of a GIS analysis can best be shown on a map. ArcMap is an excellent tool for making all kinds of maps.

Charts and reports of selected data are two other ways of presenting your results. ArcMap contains tools for making a wide variety of charts to communicate your data. ArcMap also contains a report function that lets you customize the style of the report. You can print charts and reports separately, embed them in documents created by other applications, or place them on your map.

What's next?

Now that you have reviewed the steps in a GIS project you are ready to begin planning your own project. You can get an overview of how the steps fit together with the remaining chapters in this book.

Planning your project

Throughout the rest of this book you will be working on a small GIS analysis project. You will learn to use the Desktop ArcInfo applications—ArcMap, ArcCatalog, and ArcToolbox—together and how to plan and carry out a GIS analysis project.

The City of Greenvalley is growing. To support this growth the City is building a new wastewater treatment and recycling plant. The City plans to use conservation and wastewater recycling to help meet its expected water needs. Please note that although the data used in this project is real-world data, the project is fictitious and deals with a fictitious area.

The graphic below outlines the steps in a GIS project and shows how each step is covered in the remaining chapters in this book.

Steps in a GIS project
Identify the objectives Chapter 4
Create the database Chapter 4, Chapter 5, Chapter 6, Chapter 7
Analyze the data Chapter 8
Present the results Chapter 9

As you can see, creating a GIS database is an extremely important, time-consuming part of a GIS analysis project.

Identify the objectives

Step 1: Identify the project objectives

The objective of this GIS analysis is to find a suitable site for the City's new wastewater recycling plant. The City has never used a GIS suitability model to site a wastewater treatment plant. The existing plant was sited many years ago using a quadrangle map, acetate overlays, and the City Council's knowledge of the area in consultation with the City Engineer. This approach was adequate but time consuming, and the public was not involved in the process.

The problem has become more difficult as the area has become more developed and environmental and public health regulations more stringent. The Council has chosen to use a GIS suitability model in order to speed the process and to ensure that the necessary regulations are complied with.

Because the Council recognizes that siting such a plant can be controversial, they want the analysis to identify all of the parcels that could be used for the plant site and to rank them according to their suitability. The suitable sites will be discussed at a public meeting. The map should make clear which parcels are highly suitable, which are less suitable, and which are unsuitable.

You will create the suitability model to identify the sites that meet the City's criteria. Then you will create a poster-sized map of possible site locations and a report that lists the areas of the parcels.

Create the database

Step 2: Create the project database

Creating the database for this project will be a multistep process. Fortunately, several City departments maintain GIS data and have working arrangements to share data for City projects. The City database is composed of coverages in the Universal Transverse Mercator (UTM) coordinate system.

Because a database containing much of the data you need already exists, you will not need to spend as much time on designing and automating your project database as you would otherwise. However, you will still need to do some database design work for your project database.

In this step you will need to do the following:

- Identify the data layers that you will need for the analysis and identify sources of this data.

- Manage the data to make sure that it is all in the same coordinate system.

- Identify the attributes that should be associated with the features for the analysis and add these attributes where they do not already exist.

- For those datasets that are not available in electronic form, derive the data you need from existing data or create it by digitizing.

Identify the data layers

The City has provided you with a list of the characteristics of a suitable site. The parcels chosen for the site must be

- Below 365 meters in elevation

Create the database

- Outside of the floodplain
- Within the City limits
- Within 1,000 meters of the river
- At least 150 meters from residential property

In addition, the City would prefer that the parcels be

- Within 1,000 meters of the main wastewater junction
- Within 50 meters of an existing road
- On vacant land that can be developed
- Total at least 150,000 square meters in area

Each one of these criteria will require a layer of data in the analysis. You will now take inventory of the data that you have and identify the data that you need to obtain, create, or derive.

To find areas below 365 meters elevation, you need a source of elevation data. Because you simply need to know whether or not a parcel is below 365 meters, you will use a polygon of areas below 365 meters, supplied by a colleague at the State Highway Department. This polygon has one attribute, Grid_code, that represents areas below 365 meters. The data is in a shapefile and will have to be converted to a coverage.

To find parcels outside of the floodplain, you will use the City Planning Department's digital flood zone coverage. This coverage has an attribute, flood_zone, that you will use to identify areas outside of the flood zone. Because the flood zone coverage includes the City limits, you will also be able to use this coverage to limit your selection to parcels within the City limits.

Create the database

To identify areas within 1,000 meters of the river, you will first need a coverage of the river. The County Water Resources Department has a shapefile map of the river. You will create a coverage from this shapefile; then you will create a buffer so you can identify parcels within 1,000 meters of the river.

To identify parcels that are within 50 meters of a road you will use the existing roads feature class from the GreenvalleyDB geodatabase. You will use ArcMap to select these parcels.

You will need a coverage of the parcels in your study area. The City Tax Assessor has a tiled database of parcel coverages. Two of these tiles cover your study area. The parcel database includes a land use attribute that you will use to identify parcels of vacant land. The parcels do not have a suitability attribute, so you will add one to the parcel coverage. You will also add a distance attribute that will hold a distance code for each suitable parcel. You will use the area attribute of the parcel coverage to identify parcels or sets of parcels with an area of at least 150,000 square meters.

To find parcels more than 150 meters from residential property you will start with the Tax Assessor's parcel coverage. You will derive a new coverage of residential property from this coverage; then you will create 150-meter buffers around parcels of residential land.

To find parcels within 1,000 meters of the main wastewater junction you will need a coverage that includes the junction. The City Utility Department has a coverage of the wastewater mains and the junction. You will derive the

Create the database

area within 1,000 meters of the junction from this coverage. The City Council has asked you to code the parcels within 500 meters of the junction as being close, and those parcels between 500 and 1,000 meters of the junction as being acceptable. Parcels more than 1,000 meters from the junction are too distant to be suitable.

There is a recently discovered historic site in the project area. The City plans to develop a park around the site, but the proposed park boundary has not been placed into any of the GIS databases yet. You will get this information into your project database by digitizing from a scanned image of the draft park boundary map. Parcels that intersect this park must be considered unsuitable sites for the plant.

You will gather the existing data for the analysis in the exercises in Chapter 5, 'Organizing data'.

Automate the data

Automating data involves digitizing or converting data from other systems and formats into a usable format as well as verifying the data, correcting errors, and creating topology.

Fortunately, most of the data is already in coverage, shapefile, or geodatabase format. You will now review the data that needs to be created or converted from other formats.

Two of the sets of data are in shapefile format. These must be converted to coverages. The river shapefile will need to be converted to a line coverage, and the lowland shapefile will need to be converted to a polygon coverage. You will use the Shapefile to Coverage tool from ArcToolbox to make the conversion.

Create the database

The boundary of the proposed park surrounding the historic site will need to be digitized. You have a scanned map of the proposed boundary that you will digitize using ArcMap software's editing tools. The proposed park feature will go into the existing park feature class in the GreenvalleyDB geodatabase.

You will convert the shapefiles and digitize the boundary in Chapter 6, 'Preparing data for analysis'.

Manage the database

Managing the database involves putting the spatial data into the same real-world coordinate system, joining adjacent coverages, and adding attributes to coverages where they are missing. Now you will review what needs to be done to manage the database.

The County government uses a different coordinate system than the City in their GIS database. You must be sure that all the data you use in overlay operations is in the same coordinate system. You will use the ArcToolbox Define Projection and Project wizards to place the data in the correct coordinate system.

The parcel data from the Tax Assessor is in two tiles that need to be joined together. You will use the ArcToolbox Append wizard to join these two tiles into a single coverage.

The Tax Assessor's parcel database does not include two attributes that you will need, so you will use ArcCatalog to add them to the joined parcel coverage. You will add a suitability attribute to hold the suitability values that each

Create the database

parcel receives in the model. You will also add a distance attribute to hold each parcel's distance code.

You will automate and manage the data for the analysis in the exercises in Chapter 6, 'Preparing data for analysis'.

Create derived data

Once you have got the existing data prepared for analysis, you will derive the remaining data you need from the data you have. Now you will review the data that you will derive.

You need to create several buffer areas. One coverage, the junction, will need to be buffered twice so you can identify areas that are within 500 meters of the junction, areas that are within 1,000 meters of the junction, and areas that are more than 1,000 meters of the junction. You will use the ArcToolbox Buffer tool to create these buffers. Two other coverages, the river and the residential parcels, will each need to be buffered once. These buffers will allow you to find areas within 1,000 meters of the river and parcels that are within 150 meters of residential parcels. You will use the ArcToolbox Buffer tool to create these two buffers.

Before you can buffer the residential parcels you will need to extract them from the Tax Assessor's land use coverage. You will use the Extract wizard to create a coverage of just residential parcels.

You will derive the data that does not already exist in the database in the exercises in Chapter 7, 'Creating derived data'.

Analyze the data

Step 3: Analyze the data

To analyze the data you will use attribute queries on each layer of the project database to identify areas that meet each of the City's criteria for a suitable site. You will use location queries to find parcels that are within each of these areas, and you will edit the attributes of the parcels you select to reflect their suitability.

You will also give parcels a distance code, so you can show which suitable parcels are close to the junction where the plant will connect to the existing network and which are farther away. The City Council will use this additional information when choosing the parcel for the site.

When each of the criteria has been met, you will select the most suitable parcels and create a table that shows the area and distance code of each one.

You will examine the results of your analysis, identify problems, and revise your analysis to make it better.

In Chapter 8, 'Analyzing data', you will use the project database to find suitable parcels.

Present the results

Step 4: Present the results

To present the results of the analysis you will make a final report map that shows the parcels that are suitable sites. You will include the table of parcel areas and distance codes on this map, and you will create a version of the map to go on the municipal Web site.

The results of the analysis will be presented to a general audience at a public meeting, so the map will need to clearly communicate which parcels are suitable.

You will use ArcMap to lay out the final report map.

In Chapter 9, 'Presenting your results', you will make the presentation map.

What next?

Now that you have reviewed the steps involved in a GIS project and identified the data you will need to answer the City's question, it is time to get started on the project.

You will organize the data for the project in the next chapter.

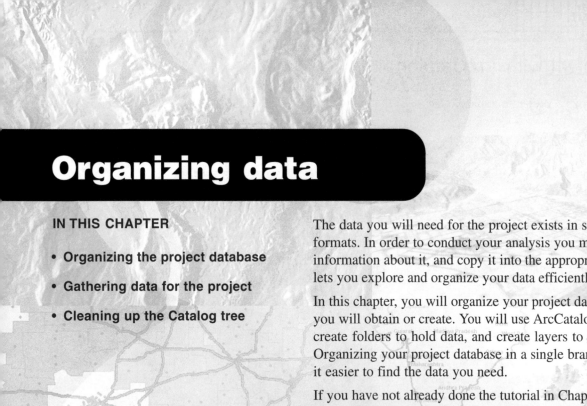

Organizing data

5

The data you will need for the project exists in several places and in different formats. In order to conduct your analysis you must find the data, get information about it, and copy it into the appropriate workspace. ArcCatalog lets you explore and organize your data efficiently.

In this chapter, you will organize your project database to hold the data that you will obtain or create. You will use ArcCatalog to preview data and copy it, create folders to hold data, and create layers to represent remote data. Organizing your project database in a single branch of the Catalog tree makes it easier to find the data you need.

If you have not already done the tutorial in Chapter 2, you will need to check with your system administrator to learn where the tutorial data is installed. Before you start the project you will also need to make a folder connection in ArcCatalog to the Greenvalley folder (use the instructions in Chapter 2).

Organizing the project with ArcCatalog

There are many ways to organize a project database. One good strategy is to create a single project folder, subfolders to hold coverage and shapefile workspaces, and a subfolder that will hold the final versions of the coverages you will use in the analysis. You can store your personal geodatabases or geodatabase connections in the project folder, or you can use layers to represent feature classes.

When you are geoprocessing coverages, it is best to work on a copy of the data so that your original data remains unmodified. In this project, the install CD contains your backup data.

Connect to the tutorial folder

Most of the folders have already been created for this project. You will copy the project folder from the Getting Started folder to your local hard drive. You will need 1 MB of disk space to store the project data. This folder represents the existing Greenvalley City database.

1. Start ArcCatalog if you have not done so already.

2. Click the Connect to Folder button.

3. Navigate to the E:\Esri\ArcTutor\Getting_Started\tutorial folder on the drive where you installed the tutorial data and click OK.

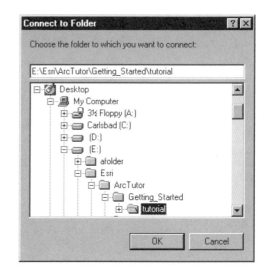

Now you can see the new folder connection in the Catalog tree.

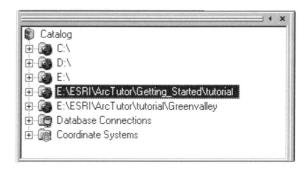

Copy the project folder

The project folder contains data that City departments are sharing with you. You will copy the project folder to your own drive to do your project.

1. Double-click the tutorial folder connection to show its contents.

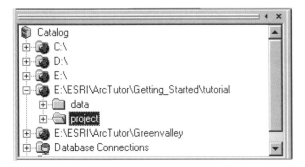

2. Click and drag the project folder from the tutorial folder connection and drop it onto your C:\ drive connection or any other local drive.

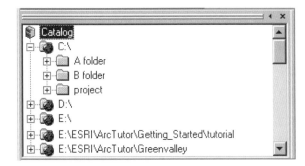

Now that you have copied the project folder to your C:\ drive, you can work on your copy of the data without modifying the City's original data.

Dragging a folder to another drive copies the folder and its contents to the new location. Dragging to another location on the same drive moves the folder. Hold the Ctrl key while you drag to copy a folder to another location on the same drive.

Connect to the project folder

If you have many folders on a drive, it can become tedious to scroll to one you use frequently. Making a connection puts that folder at your fingertips. You will do this with the project folder.

You have already made a folder connection by clicking Connect to Folder and browsing. Here is a quicker way:

1. Click C:\ in the Catalog tree to view the contents of the C:\ drive on the right side of the Catalog window.

2. Scroll to project in the Contents view, click project, and drag and drop it onto Catalog in the Catalog tree.

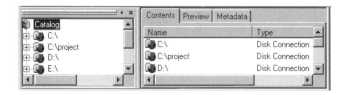

The new folder connection—C:\project is now listed in the Catalog tree.

Dragging a folder onto Catalog leaves the folder where it is in your file system but makes a connection to it in the Catalog tree.

Add folders to the project folder

The project folder only contains some of the folders and data that you will need for your project. You must add folders to the project folder to hold more data.

1. Double-click C:\project to show the contents of the folder.

The project folder contains folders called coverage, image, layer, and maps. You will add two more folders to the project folder.

2. Click File, point to New, and click Folder.

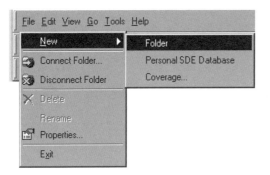

3. Repeat step 2. Now you have two new folders.

4. Click twice slowly on New Folder to rename it and type "working".

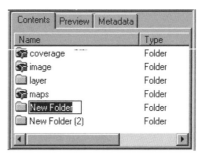

5. Click twice slowly on New Folder (2) to rename it and type "shapefile".

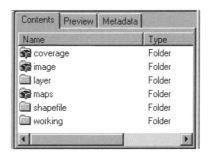

New folders are now in your project folder to store the shapefiles and coverages you will use in the final steps of the analysis.

Gathering data for the project

You have copied the coverages from the City database and added folders to organize the data from other sources. Now you will copy the data that the County and State have agreed to share.

Explore the data folder from the keyboard

You will navigate to the folders that hold the shapefiles provided by the County and State.

1. Click the Getting_Started\tutorial branch of the Catalog tree.

2. Press the down arrow key. The data folder is selected.

3. Press the right arrow key. The data folder expands to show the State_share and County_share folders.

These folders represent shared folders on a network. You can use ArcCatalog to explore any shared drive on your network for GIS data.

Examine the river shapefile

The County_share folder contains a folder called river. This folder contains a shapefile that was created by the County Water Resources Department.

1. Double-click County_share to show the folder's contents.

2. Click the river folder to view its contents on the right side of the Catalog window.

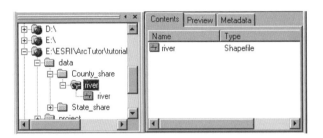

You can see that the folder contains a shapefile called river.

3. To make sure that this is the correct river, click the river shapefile in the Catalog tree and click the Preview tab.

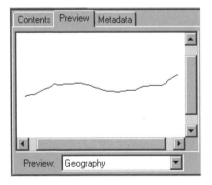

This seems to be the right river. You can check its attributes to be sure.

4. Click the dropdown arrow below the Preview window and click Table.

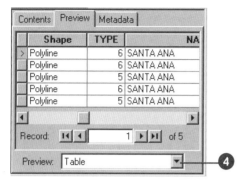

Now you can see the feature attribute table for the river shapefile.

Your project area is along the Santa Ana Wash. This is the right shapefile.

5. Click and drag the river folder and drop it on the shapefile folder in the project folder.

Your project folder now contains the river data from the County.

Examine the lowland shapefile

The State_share folder contains a folder called lowland. The lowland folder contains a shapefile created by a colleague at the State Highway Department.

1. Double-click the State_share folder and double-click the lowland folder.

2. Click the lowland shapefile.

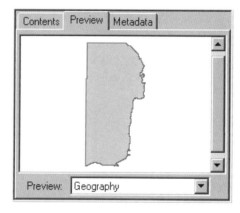

ArcCatalog detects that you have selected feature data and shows you the Geography preview.

This polygon shape defines areas below 365 meters elevation. The shapefile was made from a grid. The linear north and west edges follow the boundary of the grid. The eastern edge is irregular. You will examine this edge in greater detail.

3. Click the Zoom in button.

4. Click and drag a box around part of the eastern edge of the shape polygon.

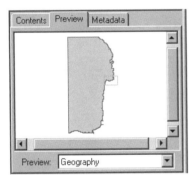

The stair-stepped edge follows the outline of the merged grid cells. This is an approximation of the 365-meter contour line.

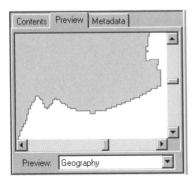

5. Click the lowland folder and drag it to the shapefile folder in the project folder.

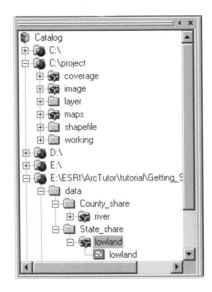

Your project folder now contains the lowland data from the State.

You have now copied most of the data you will need for the analysis project. The street and parks data that you will use is in the GreenvalleyDB geodatabase that you used in Chapter 2.

Create a streets layer

The GreenvalleyDB database is already on your local drive. Rather than create another copy of the database in the project folder, you will navigate the Catalog tree to the feature classes that you need, make layers to serve as shortcuts, and place them in the project folder.

1. Double-click the Greenvalley folder connection to show its contents.

2. Double-click Data, double-click GreenvalleyDB, then double-click Transportation.

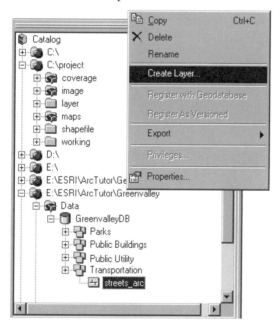

3. Right-click streets_arc, right-click the streets feature class, and click Create Layer.

4. Navigate to the layer folder in your project folder and name the layer "streets". Click Save.

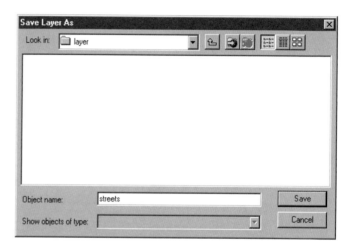

The streets layer is created in the layer folder.

Create a parks layer

Now you will use the same procedure to create a layer for the parks feature class.

1. Double-click the Parks dataset, right-click the park feature class, and click Create Layer.

2. Navigate to the Layers folder in your project folder and name the layer "parks". Click Save.

The streets and parks layers are now stored with your project data. The actual data for each layer is stored in the GreenvalleyDB database. This database is on your local drive in this case, but it could just as easily be a remote database.

Cleaning up the Catalog tree

You have made connections, created and copied folders, and created layers to organize your project database. Now the Catalog tree is beginning to appear cluttered. Before you begin working on the data, you will clean up the Catalog tree. This will make the data you need easier to find later.

Delete the connection to tutorial

The connection to the tutorial folder is unnecessary now that you have copied the project folder and the shapefiles supplied by the County and State. Deleting this connection will make more room in the tree.

1. Right-click the tutorial folder connection and click Disconnect Folder.

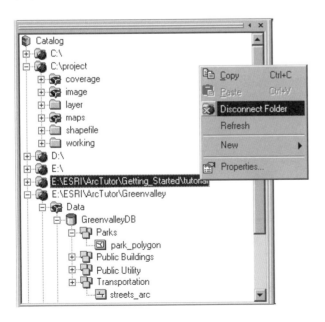

The folder connection is removed from the Catalog tree.

You will leave the conection to the Greenvalley folder so that it will be easy to add data to the database. You will do this in the next chapter.

2. Double-click the Greenvalley connection to hide its contents.

In this chapter, you have assembled the available data into an organized project database. Now the Catalog shows only the data that you need for the project. In the next chapter, you will begin preparing the data for analysis.

Preparing data for analysis

Now that you have collected and organized available data, you can make it usable for your analysis.

GIS data comes in different formats. Two of the most common are coverages and shapefiles, but many others exist. Generally, in order to use GIS data in ArcToolbox it must be in the coverage format. Fortunately, ArcToolbox comes with a wide variety of data conversion tools.

Unless GIS data is in the same coordinate system, it will not overlay correctly. ArcMap is able to match the coordinate systems of two different data sources, so you can display them together. However, for a GIS project it is a good idea to make sure that your data is all in the same coordinate system. After you put data in a new coordinate system it usually needs to have its topology rebuilt.

Coverages are sometimes stored as sets of adjacent tiles such as map sheets in a series. To do your analysis you will need to join two adjacent parcel coverages into a single set of features so you can work with all of the parcels at once.

Attributes store the characteristics of features. You can add new attributes to GIS data to store new kinds of information about a set of features. The attributes you will add will let you store the suitability and distance codes for the parcels so you will be able to retrieve the suitable parcels at the end of your analysis.

You can get geographic data into a GIS in several ways. You can buy it, get it for free off the Web, or create it by digitizing a map, scanning an image, or geolocating a table.

Introducing ArcToolbox

ArcToolbox lets you use the power of Workstation ArcInfo through a convenient Windows interface. Simple ArcInfo commands are carried out by tools. More complex commands, or sets of commands, are carried out by wizards. Most of the tools and wizards in ArcToolbox are designed to work on coverage data. Some, notably the conversion tools, will work with other types of GIS data.

Start ArcToolbox from the Start Menu

Now you will start ArcToolbox and begin to prepare your project database for analysis.

1. Click the Start button on the taskbar, point to Programs, point to ArcInfo, and click ArcToolbox.

When you start ArcToolbox, you will see four toolsets. Toolsets organize groups of tools that are used for similar purposes.

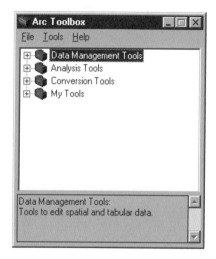

You can create your own toolsets to organize the tools that you use frequently or to group tools that you use to complete a particular task.

When you click a tool, a brief description of the tool appears at the base of the ArcToolbox window.

Changing ArcToolbox settings

Set tool dialogs to stay on top of other windows

You will perform several operations by dragging and dropping coverages onto tools. To make it easier to drag and drop from the Catalog, you can set the tool dialog boxes to always stay on top of other windows.

1. Click the Tools menu and click Options.

2. Click the check box at the bottom of the Options dialog to place tools on top. Click OK.

If you decide not to use this setting you can easily turn it off by unchecking the box.

Create a new toolset in My Tools

Toolsets let you organize the tools you use most frequently. You will create a new toolset and add the Shapefile to Coverage tool to it.

1. Right-click My Tools and point to Add toolset.

2. Type "My Conversion Tools" to name the new toolset and click OK.

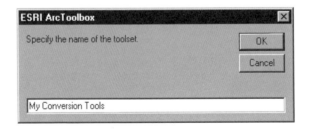

3. Double-click My Tools to view its contents.

Find a tool to add to the toolset

The new toolset, My Conversion Tools, has been added to My Tools. Now you must find the conversion tool.

1. Click Tools and click Find.

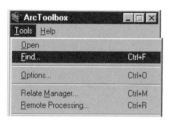

2. Type "shape" in the text box and then click Find Now.

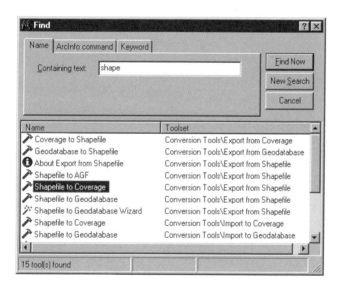

You want the Shapefile to Coverage tool.

Add the tool to the toolset

Now you can add the tool you found to your new toolset.

1. Right-click Shapefile to Coverage, point to Send to, and then click My Conversion Tools.

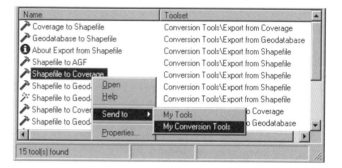

2. Close the Find dialog box and then double-click My Conversion Tools in the ArcToolbox tree.

The Shapefile to Coverage tool has been added to your toolset.

Importing shapefiles to coverages

Because you plan to use the features in these shapefiles in topological overlay operations, you will need to import the shapefiles into coverages.

If you have closed ArcCatalog since the last chapter, please restart ArcCatalog now.

Start the Shapefile to Coverage tool

1. Double-click Shapefile to Coverage in the ArcToolbox tree.

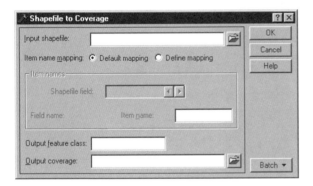

The Shapefile to Coverage dialog box opens.

2. In the project folder connection of the Catalog tree, double-click the shapefile folder and then double-click the river folder.

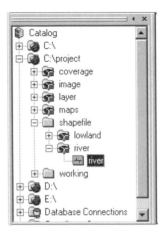

3. Click and drag the river shapefile from the Catalog tree onto the Input shapefile text box.

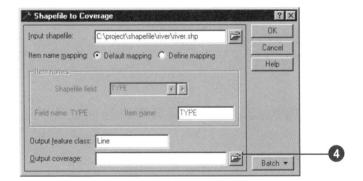

4. Click the folder button next to the Output Coverage text box.

5. In the dialog box that appears, navigate to the C:\project\coverage\river folder.

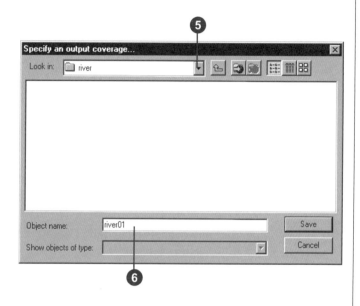

6. Type "river01" to name the new coverage. Click Save.

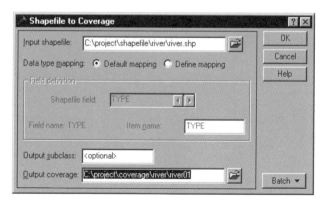

The input and output fields are now filled in correctly, and the tool is ready to run.

At this point, you could convert this shapefile to a coverage by clicking OK on the Shapefile to Coverage dialog box. However, because you have one more shapefile to convert, you will switch the tool to batch mode and add another operation. Batch mode allows you to use the same tool on several different data sources.

Most ArcToolbox tools will operate in batch mode, which can save time when you have to perform an operation on multiple coverages.

Batch mode also allows you to compose an operation with a tool, then save the operation as an AML script, and run it later.

Add an operation in batch mode

1. Click Batch on the lower-right side of the Shapefile to Coverage tool dialog box.

The Batch grid appears at the bottom of the dialog. You can use the batch grid to organize the data that you are converting.

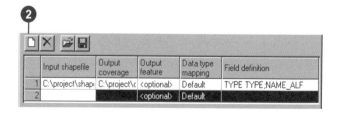

2. Click the Add Row button, located just above the Batch grid.

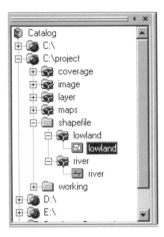

Now you can convert another shapefile with the tool.

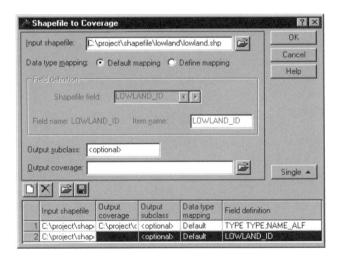

3. Double-click the lowland folder, click the lowland shapefile, and drag it onto the Input shapefile text box.

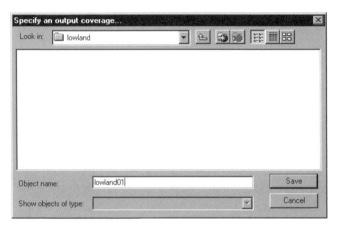

4. Click the folder button next to the Output Coverage text box.

5. Navigate to the C:\project\coverage\lowland workspace.

6. Type "lowland01" to name the new coverage. Click Save.

7. Now click OK on the Shapefile to Coverage tool dialog.

   The tool processes both of your conversion jobs.

The coverages that you have just created are not yet ready to use. The river shapefile is in the geographic coordinate system and will need to be projected into the same coordinate system as your other coverages. The lowland coverage is in the correct coordinate system, but it needs to have coordinate system information associated with it before you can use it in overlay operations.

What are coordinate systems?

ArcInfo stores features with x,y coordinates. These coordinates are linked to real-world locations by a coordinate system. The coordinate system specifies a datum and a map projection.

Datum

A *datum* is a mathematical representation of the shape of the earth's surface. A datum is defined by a spheroid, which approximates the shape of the earth and the spheroid's position relative to the center of the earth. There are many spheroids that represent the shape of the earth and many more datums based on them.

A horizontal datum provides a frame of reference for measuring locations on the surface of the earth. It defines the origin and orientation of latitude and longitude lines. A local datum aligns its spheroid to closely fit the earth's surface in a particular area; its origin point is located on the surface of the earth. The coordinates of the origin point are fixed, and all other points are calculated from this control point. The coordinate system origin of a local datum is not at the center of the earth. NAD27 and the European Datum of 1950 are local datums.

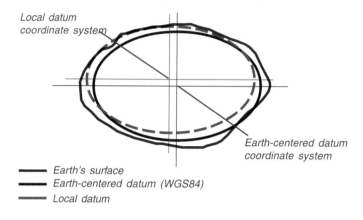

Local datum coordinate system

Earth-centered datum coordinate system

— Earth's surface
— Earth-centered datum (WGS84)
— Local datum

In the last fifteen years, satellite data has provided geodesists—mathematicians concerned with the precise measurement of the shape and size of the earth—with new measurements to define the best earth-fitting ellipsoid, which relates coordinates to the earth's center of mass. An earth-centered, or geocentric, datum does not have an initial point of origin like a local datum. The earth's center of mass is, in a sense, the origin. The most recently developed and widely used datum is the World Geodetic System of 1984 (WGS84). It serves as the framework for supporting locational measurement worldwide. Global positioning system (GPS) measurements are based on the WGS84 datum.

Map projection

Map projections are systematic transformations of the spheroidal shape of the earth so that the curved, three-dimensional shape of a geographic area on the earth can be represented in two dimensions, as x,y coordinates.

Maps are flat, but the surfaces they represent are curved. Transforming three-dimensional space onto a two-dimensional map is called 'projection'. Projection formulas are mathematical expressions that convert data from a geographical location (latitude and longitude) on a sphere or spheroid to a representative location on a flat surface. This process inevitably distorts at least one of these properties—shape, area, distance, direction—and often more.

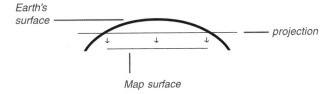

Earth's surface

projection

Map surface

Defining a coordinate system interactively

According to your colleague at the County Water Resources Department, the river shapefile is in geographic (latitude and longitude) coordinates. This means that the river01 coverage is also in the geographic coordinate system. The rest of the coverages in your project database are in the UTM coordinate system. In order to overlay the river coverage with your other coverages, you will need to define its projection for ArcInfo and then project it into the correct coordinate system.

Navigate to the projection tools

The projection tools are in the Data Management toolset.

1. In the ArcToolbox tree double-click Data Management, then double-click Projections.

Define a coordinate system

The Define Projection Wizard allows you to define the coordinate system information for a coverage.

1. Double-click Define Projection Wizard. The first panel of the wizard appears.

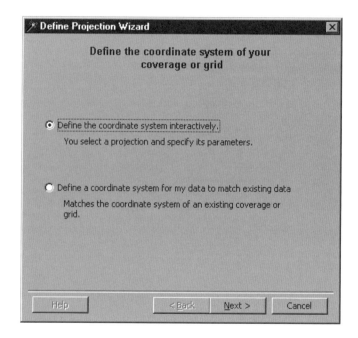

You will define the coordinate system interactively, the default, so click Next.

2. Drag the river01 coverage from the Catalog onto the Dataset text box and then click Next.

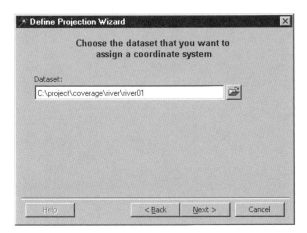

3. Select Geographic from the scrolling list of projections. Click Next.

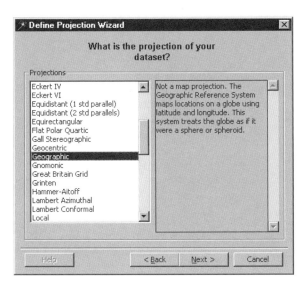

4. The Units are set to DD, Decimal Degrees. This is correct, so click Next.

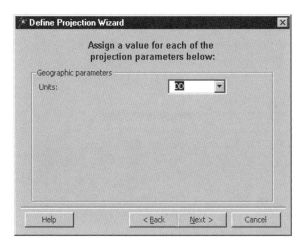

5. Click the button to select a datum, click NAD 1983 (US-NADCON), and click Next.

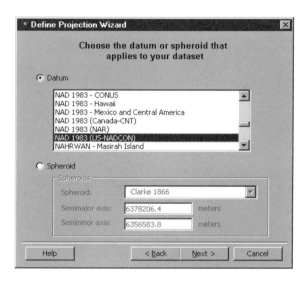

6. Review the information you gave the wizard, then click Finish.

The wizard stores the coordinates system information you have defined with the coverage. Now that the coordinate system for this coverage has been defined, you can project it to match the coordinate system of your other coverages.

Projecting a coverage

The Project Wizard lets you project a coverage interactively—specifying the new projection and datum and their associated parameters—or by matching the coordinate system of an existing coverage.

Because you have coverages that are already in the UTM coordinate system, you can simply specify the coverage to project and a coverage to match. The wizard will get the coordinate system parameters from the existing coverage.

1. Double-click Project Wizard.

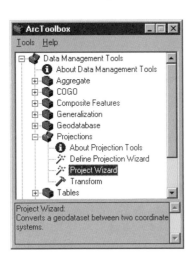

2. Click the second option to project your data to match existing data. Click Next.

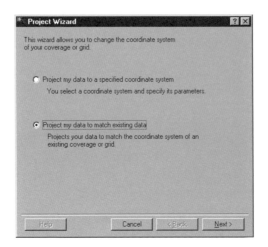

3. Drag the river01 coverage from the Catalog tree onto the Dataset text box.

The coverage name and its current coordinate system appear on the panel. Click Next.

4. Double-click flood in the Catalog tree to show its contents.

5. Click the floodzn coverage and drag it onto the match dataset text box. Click Next.

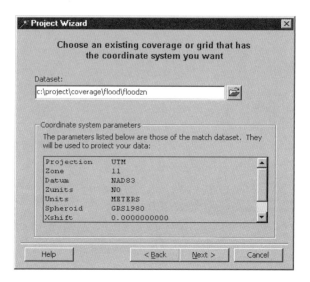

6. Type "river02" in the output Dataset text box and then press the Tab key. The path to the current workspace is added automatically. Click Next.

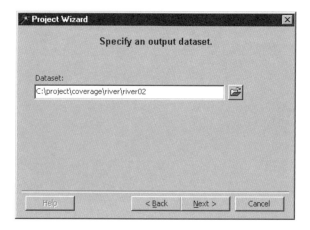

The wizard presents a summary of the input and output coordinate system parameters.

While you are still working with the projection wizards, you will define the coordinate system for the lowland coverage so you will be able to use it in overlays.

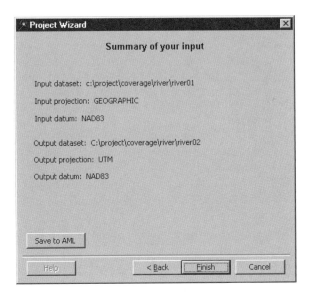

At this point you could save this projection process as an AML if you wish to run it later.

7. Click Finish on the Project Wizard dialog.

The Project Wizard projects the river coverage to match the coordinate system of the coverages in the City database. This coverage is almost ready to use.

Projecting a coverage to a new coordinate system can result in small changes in the relative positions of the features in the coverage and clipping of arcs, so topology must be reconstructed for a coverage after it is projected.

Defining a coordinate system by matching

According to your colleague at the State Highway Department, the lowland shapefile is in the UTM coordinate system. This means that the lowland01 coverage is also in the UTM coordinate system. However, the coverage does not have coordinate system information stored with it.

You will define its coordinate system for ArcInfo so you can use it in overlay operations.

Define the coordinate system

1. Double-click Define Projection Wizard in the ArcToolbox tree.

2. You will define the coordinate system by matching, so click the second option. Click Next.

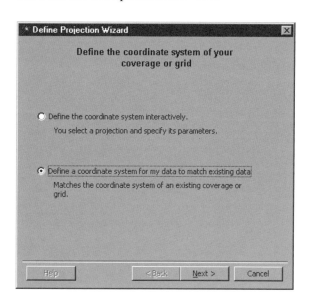

3. Double-click lowland in the Catalog tree.

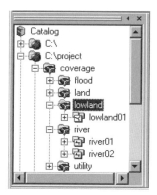

4. Drag lowland01 onto the input box of the wizard. Click Next.

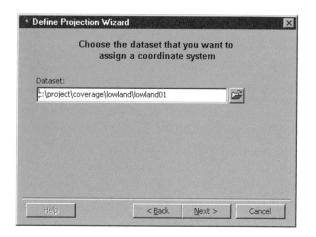

You will match the coordinate system of the river coverage that you just projected.

5. Drag the river02 coverage from the Catalog onto the match dataset box of the wizard.

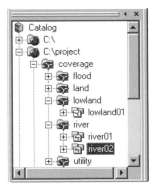

The coordinate system and parameters on the river02 coverage appear on the wizard.

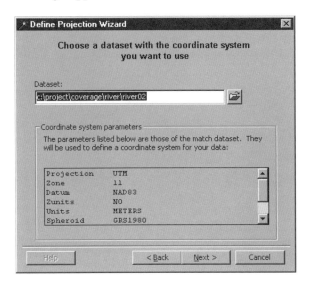

6. Click Next.

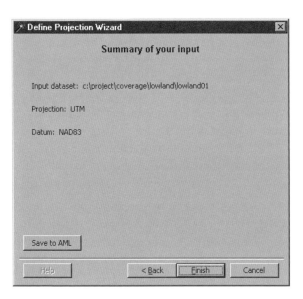

7. The wizard summarizes the projection information. Click Finish.

The coordinate system of the lowland coverage is now defined.

Because it was already in the correct coordinate system, you did not need to project the data, as you did the river coverage. ArcInfo is now able to place the features in this coverage in the correct geographic locations, relative to other features in the same coordinate system. That means that this coverage can now be used with other coverages from the City database in overlay operations.

What is coverage topology?

Coverages are the original *topological* vector data format for ArcInfo. Topology is the mathematical procedure for explicitly defining spatial relationships. The three major topological relationships that coverages maintain are connectivity, area definition, and contiguity. Storing connectivity makes coverages useful for modeling and tracing flows in linear networks. Storing information about area definition and contiguity makes it possible to find or merge adjacent polygons and to combine geographic features from different coverages with overlay operations.

Coverages store *connectivity* by recording the nodes that mark the endpoints of arcs. Arcs that share a node are connected. This is called arc–node topology. Each arc is a connected set of vertices with a from-node and a to-node.

The illustration below shows three arcs labeled 1, 2, and 3. Arc 1 starts from node 10 and goes to node 20. Its shape is defined by vertices a, b, c, and d. Arc 2 is connected to arc 1 at nodes 10 and 20.

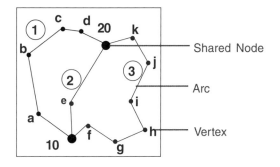

Shared Node

Arc

Vertex

Coverages *define areas* by keeping a list of connected arcs that form the boundaries of each polygon. This is called polygon–arc topology.

In this illustration polygon A is defined by arcs 1 and 2.

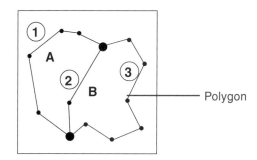

Polygon

Coverages store *contiguity* by keeping a list of the polygons on the left and right side of each arc. This is called left–right topology. Polygons that share an arc are contiguous. In this illustration polygons A and B are contiguous because A is to the left of arc 2 and B is to the right.

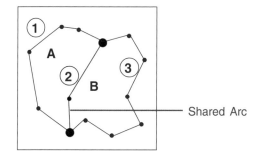

Shared Arc

Creating topology for a coverage

Coverages that you have projected or created from data in other formats often need to have topology created or reconstructed. Now that you have projected the river coverage, you will create topology for it. You will use the Clean tool in ArcToolbox to create topology.

Find the Clean tool

1. Click Tools and click Find.

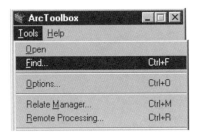

2. Type "clean" in the Find textbox and click Find Now.
3. Double-click Clean on the Find dialog box.

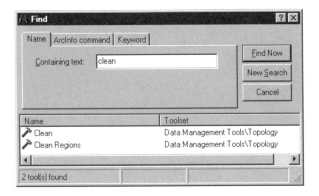

The Clean tool starts.

4. Click Cancel on the Find dialog box.

Create topology for the river coverage

The Clean tool places nodes at the intersections of arcs and builds line or polygon topology for a coverage. It is similar to the Build tool, which also constructs topology. The Build tool creates or updates a feature attribute table for point, line, polygon, node, or annotation coverages. However, the Build tool does not find intersections of overlapping arcs, which may have been created during the projection operation.

1. Drag the river02 coverage from the Catalog and drop it onto the input box of the Clean tool.

2. Click the Line Feature class button.

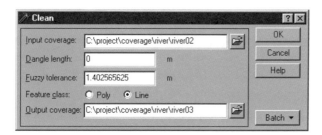

3. Click the Browse to Folder button next to the Output
   Coverage text box to browse to a workspace. Name the
   coverage "river03". Click OK.

The Clean tool creates line topology for the river03
coverage, reconnecting any arcs that may have become
disconnected in the projection process.

Appending adjacent coverages

Sometimes data that you need is in two or more adjacent coverages, either because of the way the data was created or the way it is stored. For example, multiple coverages might be created by digitizing from adjacent map sheets into separate coverages. In some cases, coverage data for large areas is stored as sets of separate tiles, where each tile is a coverage. In either case, you need to append the coverages into a single coverage in order to use them in an overlay.

The parcel data that you will use in the analysis is stored as tiles of adjacent coverages. You have two tiles that you will append into a single coverage.

Start the Append Wizard

The Append Wizard is located in the Aggregate toolset of the Data Management Tools.

1. Navigate ArcToolbox to the Append Wizard.

2. Double-click Append Wizard. The wizard starts.

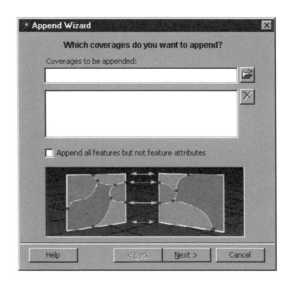

Append the two parcel coverages

1. Navigate to the land folder in the Catalog tree.

2. In the Contents view, click Parcel_1, hold the Shift key down, and click Parcel_2.

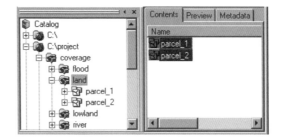

3. Drag the two selected coverages onto the Coverages to be appended text box of the Append Wizard.

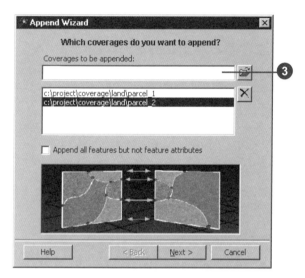

The coverages appear in the list below the text box. Click Next.

The coverages you are appending have polygon topology, and the features classes that you want to append are the polygons, since they have the land use attributes. Any attributes the line feature classes have are irrelevant to this analysis, so you will not append the line feature classes. The line geometry will be appended regardless, when you append the polygon feature classes.

4. Click Poly to append the polygon feature classes. Click Next.

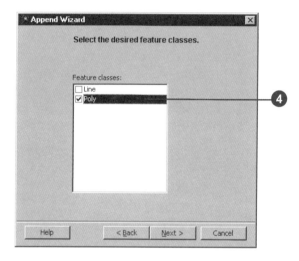

5. You will not clip the output coverage, so click Next again.

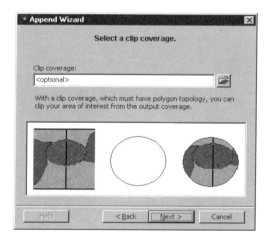

6. Click the Browse button.

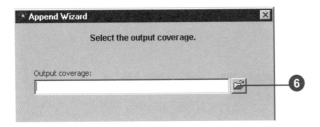

7. Navigate to the land workspace and type "parceljn01" as the output coverage name. Click Save and then click Next.

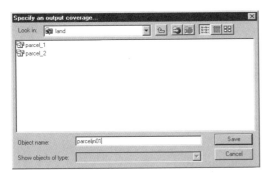

8. Click Finish on the Append Wizard dialog.

The wizard appends the two coverages.

The Append Wizard can join a series of adjacent coverages into a single coverage. In this example the coverages that were joined were tiles from a Map LIBRARIAN database. These tiles had been created by splitting a large original parcel coverage along street centerlines, so no parcel polygons crossed tile borders. In some cases polygons are split when tiles are created. For instance, a soils coverage split along census tract lines would almost certainly result in split soils polygons in separate tiles.

Had parcels been split when the tiles were created, they could be rejoined in the new coverage by using the Dissolve tool.

Adding items to a polygon attribute table

In your analysis project you will select parcels using various selection criteria. You will assign codes to the parcels to indicate how many of the criteria they satisfy or how suitable they are. You will also assign codes indicating the relative distance of a parcel from the place where the new plant will connect to the existing wastewater system. You will rank parcels as being close, distant, or too far from the junction.

You will add two items to the polygon attribute table (PAT) of the parceljn01 coverage so that you can store these attributes for each parcel.

1. In the Catalog, navigate to the polygon feature class of the parceljn01 coverage.

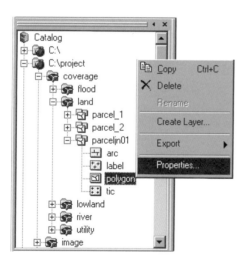

2. Right-click polygon and click Properties.

The Coverage Feature Class Properties dialog appears.

3. Click the Items tab.

4. Click Add. Click in the Item Name text box and type "SUITABLE".

5. Click the Type text box and in the dropdown list choose Integer.

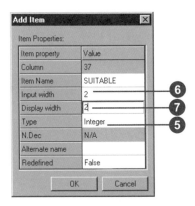

6. Click the Input width text box and in the dropdown list click 2.

7. Click the Display width text box and type "2". Click OK.

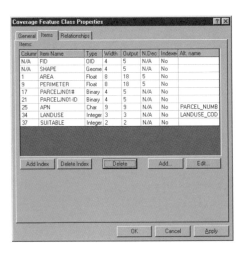

The new item, SUITABLE, is added to the attribute table of the parceljn01 polygons.

Add a second item to the attribute table

Now you will add a second attribute that will hold the distance codes.

1. Click Add on the Coverage Feature Class Properties dialog.

2. Click in the Item Name text box and type "DISTANCE".

3. Click the Type text box and in the dropdown list choose Integer.

4. Click the Input width text box and in the dropdown list click 2.

5. Click the Display width text box and type "2". Click OK.

The new item, DISTANCE, is added to the attribute table. Now you have places to store the distance and suitability codes for the parcels.

Importing a coverage to a geodatabase

You plan to select parcel features using various coverages, but you do not plan to actually overlay the parcels with other coverages. You will convert the parcel polygons from a coverage feature class into a Geodatabase feature class.

You will use ArcCatalog to put the parcel features into the GreenvalleyDB database.

1. In the Catalog, right-click the parceljn01 coverage, point to Export, then click To GeoDatabase.

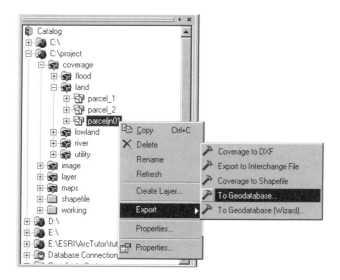

The Coverage to GeoDatabase conversion tool starts.

The input coverage is already defined on the tool. You must specify the geodatabase where you want to store the parcel polygons.

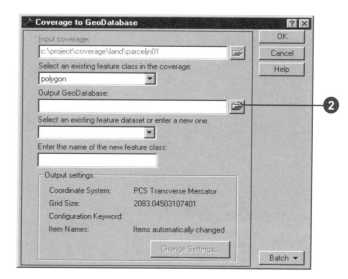

2. Click the Browse to Folder button. Navigate to the Data folder, click GreenvalleyDB, and click Open.

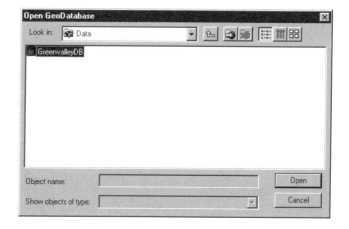

3. Type "Analysis" in the text box to create a new feature dataset.

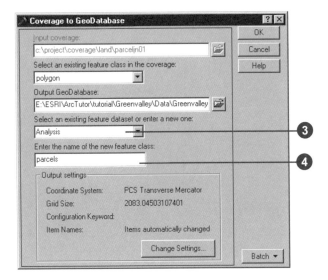

4. Type "parcels" in the text box to name the new feature class. Click OK.

The tool creates the Analysis feature dataset and stores the parcels feature class in it.

You created a new dataset in the GreenvalleyDB database to hold the new feature class. This is consistent with the organization of this geodatabase into feature datasets of thematically related feature classes.

You could also have added the feature class to one of the existing feature datasets in the geodatabase. Unlike coverages, feature datasets in geodatabases can store many feature classes with the same geometry. For example, polygon feature classes of flood zones, school districts, and parcels could be stored in the same feature dataset.

You can also store topologically related feature classes in a geodatabase if you place them in the same dataset.

Digitizing a feature

The Parks Department has not yet added the planned Homestead Historic Park to the parks features in the GreenvalleyDB database, though they have settled on the boundary. You will digitize the park boundary from a scanned image of the map.

Open the Digitize map and add a layer

You will use the Editor to digitize a new feature into the Parks feature class in the GreenvalleyDB.

1. In the Catalog, navigate to maps folder of the project database and double-click the Digitize map.

2. In ArcMap, click the Editing Toolbar button to add the Editing toolbar to ArcMap.

Editing Toolbar button

The Editing toolbar appears.

3. In the Catalog, double-click the layer folder, click parks, and drag it onto the map.

You can see in the table of contents that this map has three layers: historic.tif, park_polygon, and parcel_2 polygon.

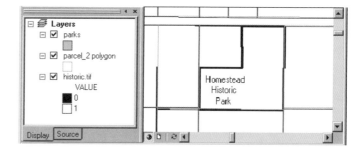

The TIF file, historic.tif, is a scanned image of the park boundary map. It has been registered to approximately the same coordinate system as the Greenvalley City database.

You will align the feature that you add to the parks polygon layer exactly with the surveyed parcel boundaries by snapping to the parcel_2 polygon layer.

Prepare to digitize the park boundary

1. Click Editor and click Start Editing.

The Start Editing dialog appears. You want to add a feature to the parks polygon feature class, so you will choose to edit in the GreenvalleyDB workspace.

2. Click the second workspace to edit features in the GreenvalleyDB geodatabase. Click OK.

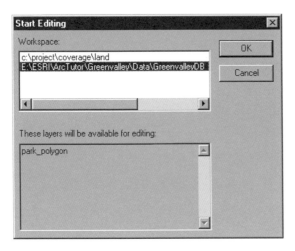

The Editor toolbar shows that you are editing the park_polygon feature class,

and the current editing task is Create New Feature.

Now you will set the snapping environment so the new park boundary will align with the existing parcel boundaries.

3. Click Editor, then click Snapping.

4. Check the box in the Vertex column for the parcel_2 polygon layer. This will snap the editing cursor to the vertices of the parcels. Leave the Snapping Environment dialog box open.

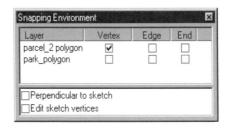

The snapping tolerance defines how close the cursor must be to an object before it snaps to that object. You can change the snapping tolerance by choosing Options from the Editing menu. For this exercise you do not need to change the snapping tolerance.

Start digitizing the park boundary

1. Click the Sketch tool.

If you make a mistake while digitizing, click the Undo Last Action button on the ArcMap standard toolbar.

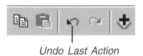

Undo Last Action

It may help you to zoom in to the northeast corner of the park—you can use the pan and zoom tools while you are digitizing. Just click the zoom tool, drag a rectangle around the area you want to see, and click the sketch tool again to resume digitizing.

2. Move the editing cursor over the northeast corner of the Homestead Historic Park boundary.

The existing parcel boundaries are drawn with light blue lines, and the park boundary is drawn with a heavy black line. When the cursor gets within the snapping tolerance of the parcel corner, the blue dot snaps to the vertex.

3. Click the northeast corner of the park to start your edit sketch.

4. Move the cursor to the southeast corner of the park. There are two vertices here. Make sure that the cursor snaps to the southernmost vertex. Click the vertex.

After you add the second point, the Editor draws a line back to the first point in your sketch to complete the polygon.

5. Move the cursor to the southwest corner of the park. There are two vertices here. Click the southernmost vertex.

Place a sketch vertex by angle and distance

This segment of the park boundary is only half as long as the parcel boundary. You will place the next point using angle and distance.

1. Place the cursor near the parcel boundary line at the corner of the park. Right-click and click Parallel.

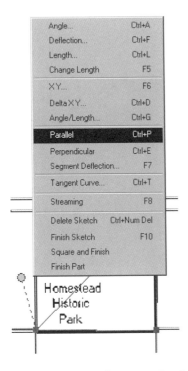

Now the cursor is constrained to be parallel to the parcel boundary.

2. Right-click again and click Angle/Length.

The Angle/Length dialog appears.

3. Click in the Length text box and type "97.78". This is half the length of the parcel boundary. Press the Enter key.

Construct another parallel segment

1. Move the editing cursor near the midpoint of the north boundary of the parcel. Right-click and click Parallel.

   Now the next segment that you add will be parallel to the north boundary of the parcel.

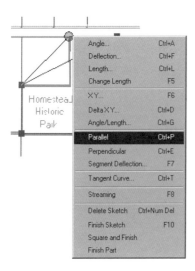

2. Right-click again and click Angle/Length. Type "100.5"and press Enter.

   The new segment is added to the edit sketch; it is 100.5 meters long and parallel to the north boundary of the parcel.

Add a perpendicular line

1. On the Snapping Environment dialog box, check Perpendicular to sketch. Now the cursor will snap to an imaginary line that is perpendicular to the last segment you added.

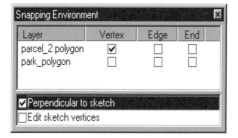

2. Move the editing cursor along the perpendicular line, partway to the north boundary of the parcel. Click to add a point.

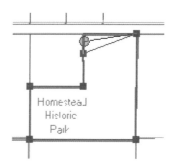

Add a point at the intersection of lines

1. Click the Sketch tool dropdown arrow and click the Intersection tool.

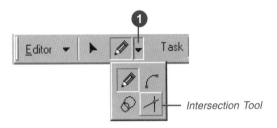

Intersection Tool

The Intersection tool lets you place the next point in your edit sketch at the intersection of two lines.

2. Place the crosshair cursor near the segment you just created. An imaginary line extends along the segment. You will make this the first intersection line. Click to set the intersection line.

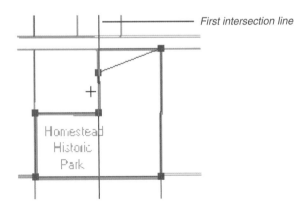

First intersection line

3. Place the crosshair cursor near the north boundary of the parcel. You will make this the second intersection line. Click to set the intersection line.

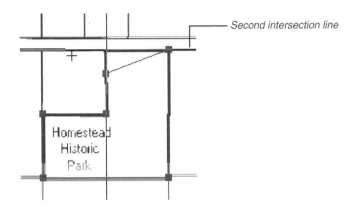

Second intersection line

The new point appears at the intersection of the north–south line that you sketched and the existing parcel boundary line.

Finish the editing sketch

1. Click the northeast corner of the park, right-click, and then click Finish Sketch.

The new park polygon is finished. Its boundary turns light blue to indicate that it is selected, and it takes on the color of the other park polygons.

Edit feature attributes

Now that you have finished sketching the park, you can update the new feature's attributes in the database.

1. Click the Attributes tool.

2. Type "Historic Park" as the value for the Name field.

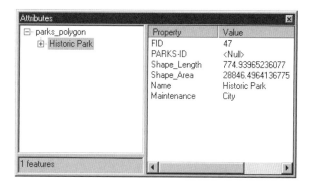

The park will be maintained by the City, so you will update the maintenance field as well.

3. Type "City" as the value for the Maintenance field. Close the Attributes dialog.

Save your changes

Now save your changes to the park feature class in the database.

1. Click Editor, then click Save Edits.

2. Click Editor, then click Stop Editing.

You have created a new feature by digitizing from a scanned image and added some attributes to it. Although this was a simple example, you saw how the Editor can be used to construct features.

In this chapter you have prepared your data for the analysis. Preparing data—whether by converting it, changing its coordinate system, managing its attributes, or editing its features—is a very important part of a GIS project. An organization's biggest investment in a GIS project, other than its staff, is usually in its data.

Creating derived data

IN THIS CHAPTER

- **Extracting polygons from a coverage**

- **Buffering coverages**

- **Erasing coverages**

- **Overlaying coverages**

Now almost all of the data you need for the analysis is ready; it is in a common coordinate system, the parcels have items for their distance and suitability, and you have added the parcels and Historic Park to your database.

In this chapter, you will derive the remaining data you need for the analysis from the data that you have acquired and prepared. You will continue to use ArcToolbox and ArcCatalog to complete this work.

So you will not choose parcels within 150 meters of a residential parcel for the plant site, you will create a new coverage by extracting residential land polygons from the land use coverage. You will use this coverage to create buffer zones around residential parcels.

Next, to allow you to select parcels that are within 1,000 meters of the river, you will buffer the river. You will also buffer the junction where the plant will connect to the wastewater system, so you can rank plant sites according to their distance from the junction.

Next, to reduce the number of selections you will have to make during the analysis, you will erase the buffered residential parcels from the lowland coverage.

Finally, to reduce the number of layers you will have to use in the analysis, you will overlay (spatial join) the flood zone coverage with the buffer zone around the river.

When you have finished these steps, you will be ready to analyze the data.

Extracting polygons from a coverage

The parceljn01 coverage you created by joining the Tax Assessor's parcel tiles contains land use attribute codes. Because the plant must be located at least 150 meters from residential parcels, you will create a new coverage of residential parcels and then buffer that coverage. You will use the Extract Wizard in ArcToolbox to extract the residential parcel polygons into a new coverage of residential parcels.

Start the Extract Wizard

The Extract Wizard is in the Extract toolset in the Analysis tools.

1. Navigate ArcToolbox to the Extract Wizard.

2. Double-click Extract Wizard.

Extract the residential parcels

1. Click Area features. Click Next.

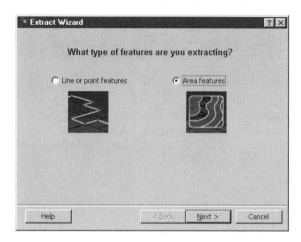

2. Click the first option. Click Next.

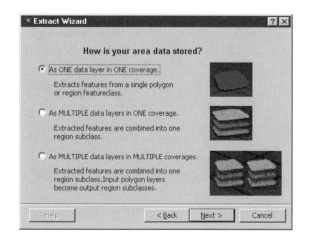

3. In ArcCatalog, navigate to the land workspace of the coverage folder.

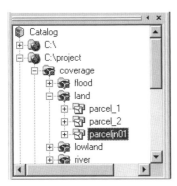

4. Click and drag the parceljn01 coverage onto the Input coverage text box of the Extract Wizard. Click Next.

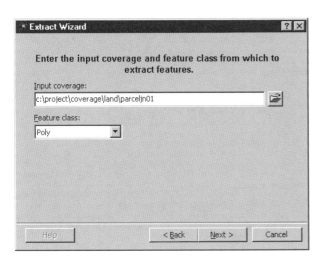

5. Click Build a query.

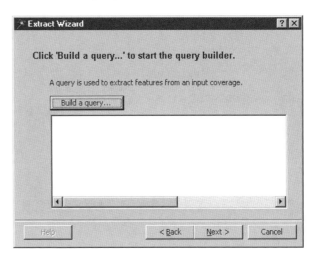

The Query Builder dialog box appears. You can use the Query Builder to create complex, multistep attribute queries on coverages. The Extract Wizard and several other ArcToolbox wizards use these queries to select specific features.

After you have extracted the residential parcels you will buffer them as described later in this chapter.

Build a query

You will use the Query Builder to create a simple query expression. The Extract Wizard will use this expression to extract the polygon features that are residential land.

1. Click LANDUSE in the Items list.

2. Click the equals sign (=) in the Operators list.

3. Click 510 in the Values list. The code for residential land is 510 in the Assessor's database.

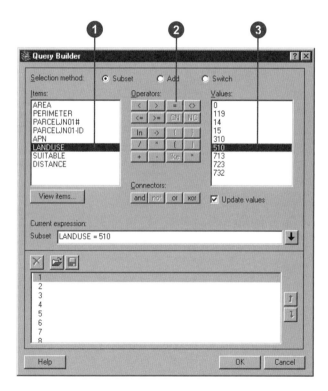

You can see the query expression you have built in the Current Expression text box.

4. Click the down arrow to add the expression to the Query expression list and then Click OK.

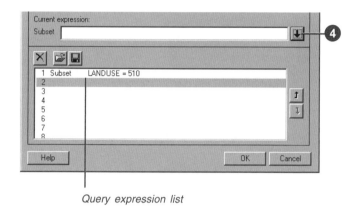

Query expression list

5. Click Next.

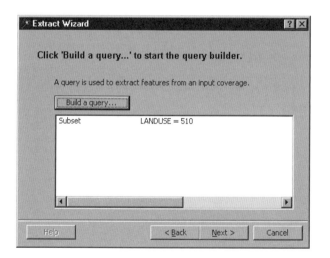

6. Click Browse and navigate to the Land workspace.

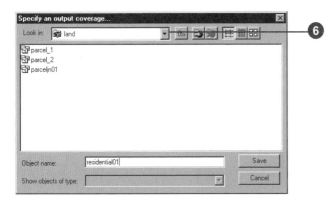

7. Type "residential01" to name the output coverage. Click Save.

8. Click Next.

9. The Extract Wizard gives you a summary of your choices. Click Finish.

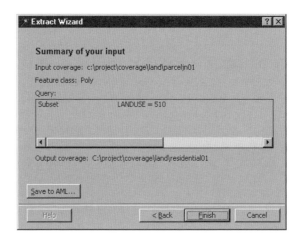

10. The wizard offers you a summary of its results. Click No.

You have created a new coverage of residential parcels. Now you will be able to make buffers to keep the plant from being sited too close to a residence.

You are creating buffers of three coverages for this analysis. In the next exercises, you will use the Buffer Wizard to create multiple buffers on a single coverage and the Buffer tool to create single buffers around two different coverages.

Buffering with the ArcToolbox Buffer Wizard

The junction coverage contains the main wastewater junction point where the new plant will connect to the existing system.

You will use the Buffer Wizard in ArcToolbox to create a new coverage containing two buffer zones around this point. You will use these zones to rank parcels according to their distance from the junction.

Start the Buffer Wizard

The Buffer Wizard is in the Proximity toolset of the Analysis tools.

1. Navigate to the Buffer Wizard.

2. Double-click Buffer Wizard.

Buffer the junction coverage

1. The first panel of the Buffer Wizard appears. Click Next.

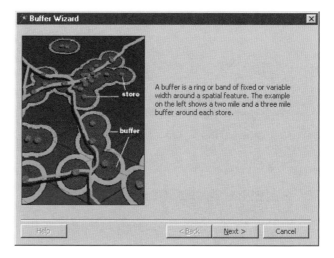

2. In ArcCatalog, navigate to the utility workspace in the coverage folder.

3. Click and drag the junction coverage onto the input text box of the Buffer Wizard. Click Next.

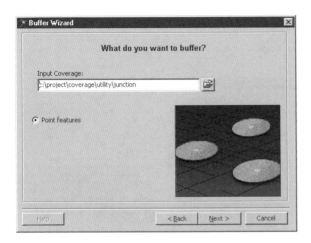

4. Click the first option to store the buffer areas in a new polygon coverage. Click Next.

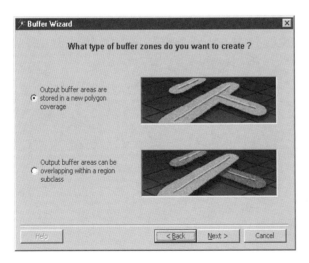

5. Click the third option to create multiple fixed-width buffer zones. Click Next.

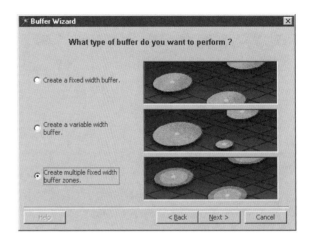

6. You will create a 500- and a 1,000-meter buffer around the junction. Type "500" in the Distance 1 text box and "1000" in the Distance 2 text box. Click Next.

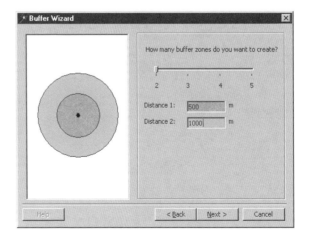

7. Click Browse and navigate to the working folder in the project folder. Type "juncbuf01" to name the coverage. Click Save.

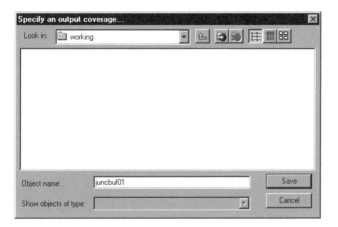

8. Type "Distance" to name the item in the coverage attribute table.

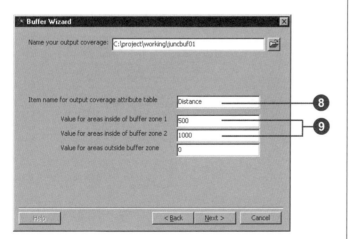

9. Type "500" as the value for areas inside buffer zone 1, and type "1000" as the value for areas inside buffer zone 2. Click Next.

10. The Buffer Wizard presents you with a summary of your choices. Click Finish.

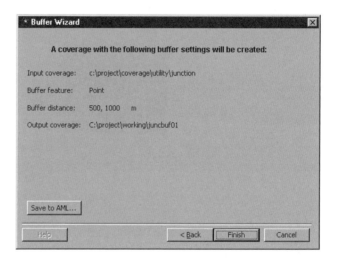

The Buffer Wizard creates a new coverage of the two derived buffer zones.

Now you can use these zones to select parcels in the analysis so you can code candidate parcels according to their distance from the main junction.

Buffering with the ArcToolbox Buffer tool

Now you need to derive buffer zones around the residential parcels and the river. You will use the Buffer tool in batch mode to complete both tasks quickly.

Start the Buffer tool

The Buffer tool is in the Proximity toolset of the Analysis Tools toolset.

1. Navigate to the Buffer tool.

2. Double-click Buffer tool.

Buffer the residential parcels

The residential parcels have been extracted into the residential01 coverage. In this step, you will create the 150-meter buffer around residential parcels.

1. In the Catalog, navigate to the land workspace of the coverage folder. Click the residential01 coverage and drag and drop it onto the Input coverage text box of the Buffer tool.

2. Type "150" in the Distance text box.

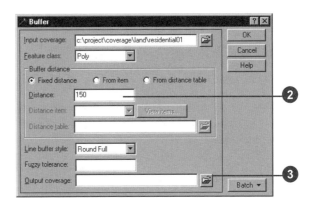

3. Click the Browse button.

4. Navigate to the land workspace. Type "resbuf02" to name the output buffer coverage and click Save.

At this point, you could run the Buffer tool to buffer the residential parcels. Before you do, you will switch to batch mode and add the river coverage.

Buffer the river in batch mode

The river coverage must be buffered so that you can site the plant within 1,000 meters of the river.

1. Click Batch.

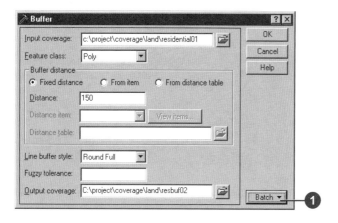

The batch grid appears at the bottom of the Buffer dialog. Now you can add a row for the river coverage.

2. Click the Add Row button.

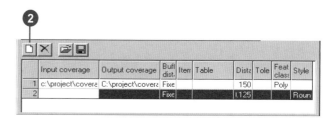

3. In the Catalog, navigate to the river workspace. Click and drag the river02 coverage onto the Input coverage text box of the Buffer tool.

4. Type "1000" in the Distance text box.

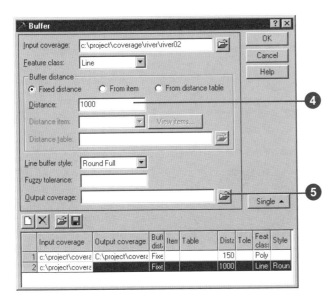

5. Click the Browse button.

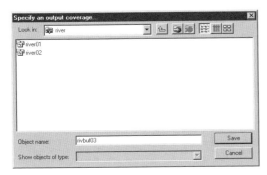

6. Navigate to the river workspace. Type "rivbuf03" to name the river buffer coverage. Click Save.

7. Click OK on the Buffer dialog.

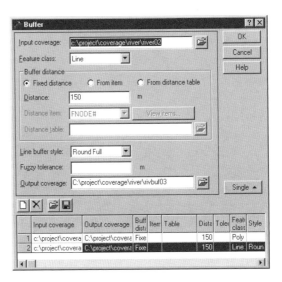

The Buffer tool creates buffers around the residential parcels and the river and saves the output buffer coverages in their respective workspaces.

Now you will be able to select parcels that are more than 150 meters from residential land and also those that are within 1,000 meters of the river.

Erasing areas from a coverage

To reduce the number of selections to make during the analysis, you will combine information from the lowland01 and resbuf02 coverages.

Parcels for the plant site must be completely inside the area defined by the lowland01 coverage, and they must be completely outside of the areas defined by the resbuf02 coverage. You will use the Erase tool to remove the areas where the two overlap from the lowland01 coverage. You will then be able to use the resulting coverage to select parcels that are both below 365 meters in elevation and more than 150 meters from a residential parcel.

Start the Erase tool

The Erase tool is in the Overlay toolset of the Analysis Tools toolset.

1. Navigate to the Erase tool.

2. Double-click Erase to start the tool.

Erase areas from a coverage

1. In the Catalog navigate to the lowland workspace.

2. Click and drag the lowland01 coverage and drop it onto the Input coverage text box of the Erase tool.

3. Navigate the Catalog to the land workspace.

4. Click and drag the resbuf02 coverage and drop it on the Erase coverage text box.

5. Click the Browse button to name the output coverage.

6. Navigate to the working workspace and type "loresbuf01" to name the output coverage. Click Save.

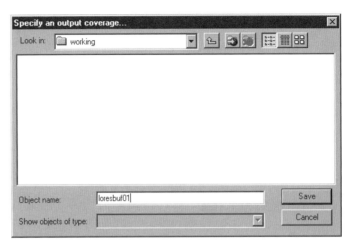

7. Click OK to erase the areas of overlap from the output coverage.

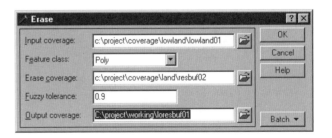

The Erase tool removes the areas where residential buffers overlap the lowland polygon.

The loresbuf01 coverage will allow you to select parcels that are completely below 365 meters in elevation and that are more than 150 meters from a residential parcel.

Overlaying coverages with the Overlay Wizard

To reduce the number of layers from which you will be selecting during the analysis, you will combine the juncbuf01 coverage and the floodzn coverage.

Start the Overlay Wizard

The Overlay Wizard is in the Overlay toolset in the Analysis Tools toolset.

1. Navigate ArcToolbox to the Overlay Wizard.

2. Double-click Overlay Wizard.

Overlay two coverages

1. On the first panel of the Overlay Wizard, click the second option to combine the features inside the area of the first coverage (Identity). Click Next.

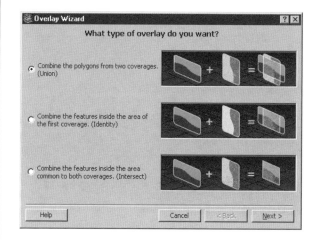

2. In the Catalog, navigate to the flood workspace.

3. Click and drag the floodzn coverage onto the Input coverage text box. Click Next.

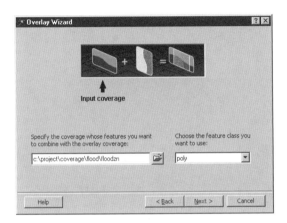

4. In the Catalog, navigate to the river folder.

5. Click and drag the rivbuf03 coverage onto the Overlay coverage text box. Click Next.

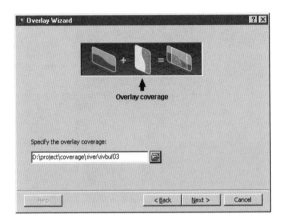

6. Click the first option to keep all attributes from both coverages. Click Next.

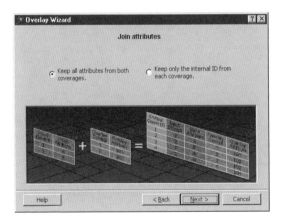

7. Click the Browse button and navigate to the working folder. Type "rivflood01" to name the output coverage. Click Save.

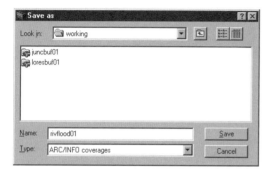

8. Click Next.

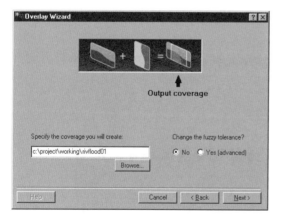

The Overlay Wizard gives you a summary of your choices.

9. Review the summary, then click Finish.

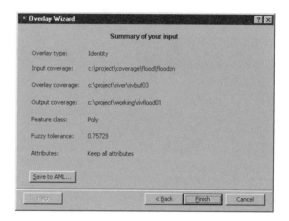

The Overlay Wizard merges the two coverages into a single coverage.

Now you can use the rivflood01 coverage to select parcels that are within 1,000 meters of the river but outside of the flood zone.

In this chapter you have created new data by extracting, buffering, erasing, and overlaying your existing data. These operations are representative of the many key GIS functions you can perform with ArcToolbox.

In the next chapter, you will use the project database, including the new data you have created, to find the most suitable parcels for the wastewater recycling plant.

Analyzing data

8

IN THIS CHAPTER

- **Selecting features**

- **Editing feature attributes**

- **Symbolizing a layer**

- **Examining summary statistics**

In this chapter, you will use a suitability model to identify the parcels that meet the City of Greenvalley's selection criteria.

This suitability model has two levels of importance: mandatory and preferred criteria. It is important to the City that the selected parcels meet all of the mandatory criteria, so these criteria are given more weight in the analysis. This ensures that if a parcel fails to meet one of the mandatory criteria, it will not be classified as suitable, regardless of how many other criteria it meets.

You will start by adding the parcel feature class to a new map. You will then use data you have derived to find parcels that meet the City's five mandatory criteria. You will give parcels that meet the City's mandatory criteria extra points in your analysis.

Once you have identified the minimally suitable parcels, you will find parcels that meet the City's preferred criteria and increase those parcels' suitability values. When you have finished, you will be able to select the parcels with the highest suitability codes—the best places to put the plant.

You could also create a suitability model where all of the criteria had the same importance. For example, if the City were equally concerned that the parcel be close to a road and distant from a residence, each could be given equal weight in the model.

Starting a new map

Now that you have collected or derived the data you need, it is time to start the analysis. You will use a new map to do the analysis.

Launch ArcMap

If you have closed ArcMap since you digitized the historic park, you can use the Launch ArcMap button in ArcCatalog to start ArcMap.

1. In ArcMap, click File and click New.

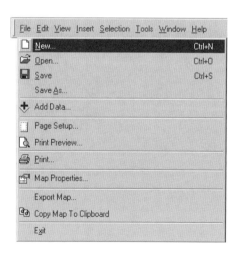

2. Click the normal template. Click OK.

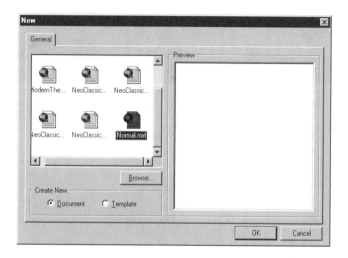

ArcMap asks whether you want to save your edits.

3. You do not need to save the changes that you made to the Digitize map because you have already saved the changes to the park_poly feature class. Click No.

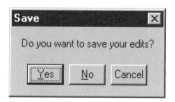

Add data to the map

1. In the Catalog tree, navigate to the Analysis dataset in GreenvalleyDB.

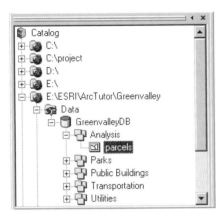

2. Click parcels and drag it onto the map.

The parcels feature class is drawn on the map.

3. In ArcCatalog navigate to the working folder.

4. Click loresbuf01 and drag it onto the map.

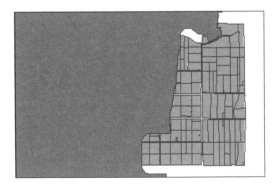

The parcels that are below 365 meters in elevation and more than 150 meters from residential land are hidden by the new layer.

Selecting with all features in a layer

Now that you have the parcels and the loresbuf01 polygon on the map, you can begin your analysis. To start, you will select the parcels that fall within the loresbuf01 polygons. You can see the outlines of the buffers around residential parcels as rounded rectangles, erased from the edge of the lowland area.

Select parcels

Now you will select by location the parcels that are within the loresbuf01 polygon—they are below 365 meters and more than 150 meters from residential land.

1. Click Selection and click Select By Location.

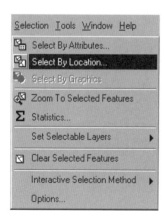

The Select By Location dialog box appears. This dialog box lets you compose a wide variety of location queries.

2. Check the box to select parcels.

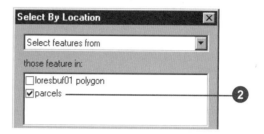

3. Click the dropdown arrow to choose a new type of selection. Click "are completely within".

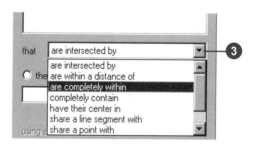

4. Click the option to select using all features.

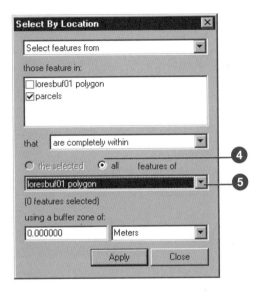

5. Click the dropdown arrow and click loresbuf01 polygon.

6. Click Apply. ArcMap selects the parcels that are completely within the loresbuf01 polygon.

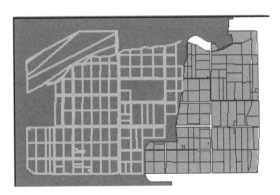

This selection does not include parcels that are partly below 365 meters.

You could have selected parcels that intersected the loresbuf01 polygon, which would have included more parcels, but for this analysis the current selection is suitable.

7. Click Close to close the Select By Location dialog box.

Start editing

You have now selected the parcels that meet two of the City's criteria: they are below 365 meters in elevation, and they are more than 150 meters from a residential parcel. You will set the value of the attribute "suitable" to 5 for these parcels.

1. Click Editor and click Start Editing.

The Start Editing dialog box appears. You will choose the workspace that you will be editing.

2. Click the E:\ESRI\ArcTutor\Greenvalley\Data\
GreenvalleyDB.mdb workspace path. Click OK.

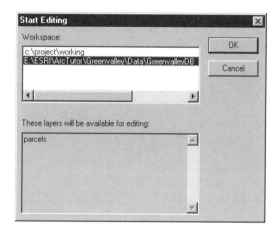

Now you will be able to edit the parcels you have
selected.

Open the Attributes dialog box

One way to edit the attributes of a feature—or a group of
selected features—is through the Attributes dialog box. You
will use this method to update the SUITABLE attribute of
the selected parcels.

1. Click the Attributes button.

Attributes

The Attributes dialog box appears.

The dialog box indicates that 151 features are selected.

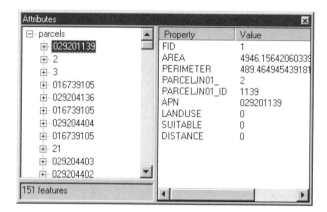

You can view and edit any attribute of any of these
features by selecting the feature from the list on the left
side of the dialog box, clicking the appropriate cell in the
Value column, and typing a value.

2. Click parcels at the top of the list of selected parcels.

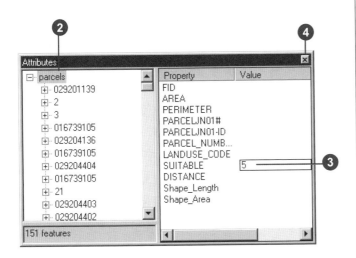

Now you can update an attribute for all of the selected features.

3. Type "5" in the Value column next to SUITABLE. Press the Enter key.

ArcMap updates the SUITABLE attribute with the value 5 for the selected parcels.

4. Click the Close button to close the dialog box.

5. Click Editor and click Save Edits.

Each parcel that is both below 365 meters in elevation and more than 150 meters from a residential parcel now has a value of 5 to indicate that it meets this set of the City's mandatory criteria.

Remove the loresbuf01 layer

Now that you have updated the suitability rank for these parcels you no longer need the loresbuf01 layer on the map. You will remove it from the map.

1. In the table of contents, right-click loresbuf01 polygon. Click Remove.

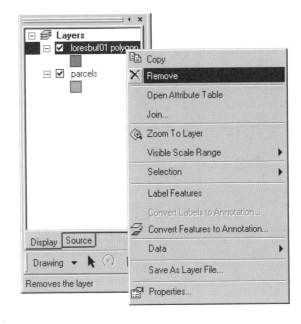

ArcMap removes the layer from the map. You are ready to find parcels that meet the next set of mandatory criteria.

Selecting with selected features

You will now select parcels that meet three more of the City's mandatory criteria. You will use the rivflood01 coverage to find areas that are within 1,000 meters of the river, outside of the flood zone, and within the City limits.

Add the rivflood01 polygons

First you will need to add the rivflood01 coverage to the map.

1. In the Catalog, click rivflood01 and drag it onto the map.

The rivflood01 polygons are drawn on the map, almost completely covering the parcel polygons.

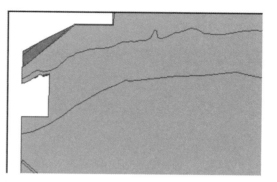

Select polygons by their attributes

You are going to select the areas of the rivflood01 coverage that are within the river buffer and outside of the flood zone.

1. Click Selection and click Select By Attributes.

The Select By Attribute dialog appears.

2. Click the Layer dropdown arrow and click rivflood01 polygon.

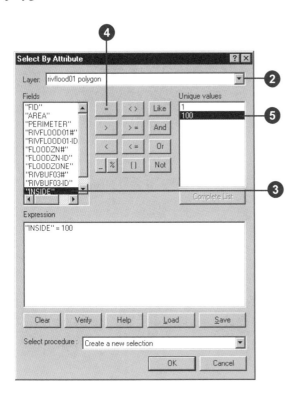

3. Double-click "INSIDE" in the Fields list.

4. Click the equals sign (=).

5. Double-click 100 in the Unique values list.

The query expression appears in the expression box. This expression will select all polygons from the coverage that have the value of 100 for the INSIDE field—the polygons inside the river buffer.

Add to the query expression

You want the query to select the polygons that are also outside the flood zone.

1. Click And.

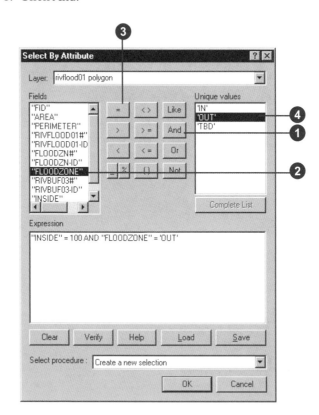

2. Double-click "FLOODZONE" in the Fields list.

3. Click the equals sign.

4. Double-click 'OUT'. Review the query expression to make sure it is correct. Click OK.

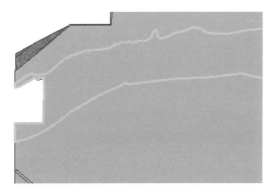

ArcMap processes the query and selects the polygons that are both inside the river buffer and outside the flood zone.

Select by location

Now you can use the selected polygons to find parcels that meet these two criteria. Because the coverage is bounded by the City limits, the parcels you select will also be within the City limits.

1. Click Selection and click Select By Location.

The Select By Location dialog box appears. The parcels layer should already be checked on.

2. Click the dropdown arrow to choose a selection type and click "are completely within".

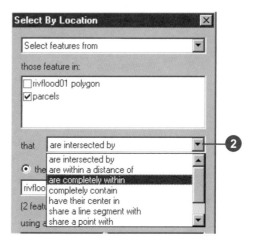

Because you have some features selected in the rivflood01 polygon layer, the dialog box defaults to selecting by the selected features.

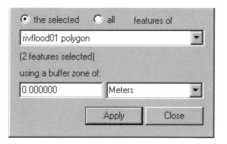

3. Click Apply.

ArcMap selects the parcels that are within the two selected polygons.

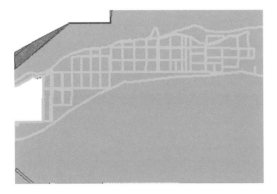

4. Click Close to close the Select By Location dialog box.

Update the suitability code

These parcels meet the other three of the City's mandatory criteria. You will add 5 to their suitability codes.

1. In the ArcMap table of contents, right-click the parcels layer and click Open Attribute Table.

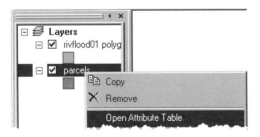

The Attributes window appears. The selected features are highlighted in yellow.

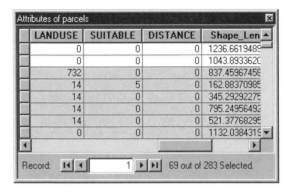

2. Scroll to the SUITABLE column of the table.

3. Right-click SUITABLE and click Calculate Values.

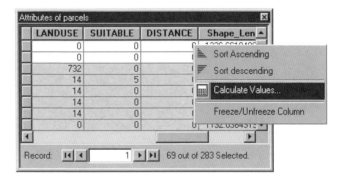

The Field Calculator dialog box appears. You can change the values of selected features with the Field Calculator.

4. Click SUITABLE in the Field list.

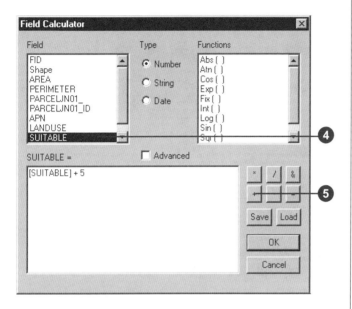

5. Click the plus sign and type the number "5".

6. Review the expression in the Calculator window and then click OK.

The value 5 is added to the current value in the SUITABLE field of each selected feature. Now some parcels have a suitability code of 10, while others have values of 0 or 5. This is different from the Editor's Attributes dialog box, which allows you to enter a new value for an attribute of a feature but does not do computations with the values.

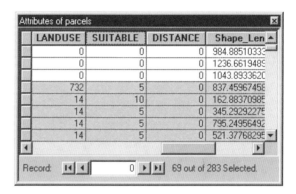

You can use the Field Calculator to compose calculations using multiple fields. For example, you could calculate cost per square meter of selected parcels by dividing an area field by a price field.

7. Click Editor and click Save Edits.

Remove the rivflood01 layer

Now that you have updated the suitability value for these parcels, you can remove rivflood01 from the map.

1. In the ArcMap table of contents, right-click rivflood01 polygon. Click Remove.

The parcels that meet all five of the City's mandatory criteria have suitability values of 10. This score is the cutoff point for parcels to be eligible for further consideration as sites for the plant. Any parcel with a score of less than 10 is necessarily unsuitable, regardless of how many of the City's preferred criteria it meets.

In the next steps, you will find the parcels that meet the City's preferred criteria. You will add one point to the suitability score for each of the preferred criteria a parcel meets.

Updating distance and suitability

The City would prefer that the plant site be within 1,000 meters of the point where the plant will connect to the existing wastewater system. The council is willing to accept parcels that extend beyond the 1,000-meter buffer as long as most of the parcel is within the buffer.

Add the juncbuf01 polygons

First you will add the juncbuf01 coverage to the map.

1. In ArcCatalog, navigate to the working folder.

2. Click juncbuf01 and drag it onto the map.

   The two concentric buffer polygons are added to the map.

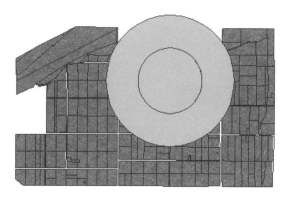

Select parcels by location

This time you will use another selection technique to select parcels where the parcel's center falls within the 1,000-meter buffer.

1. Click Selection and click Select By Location.

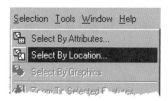

The Select By Location dialog box appears.

2. Click the dropdown arrow to choose to select parcels that "have their center in" the features of juncbuf01.

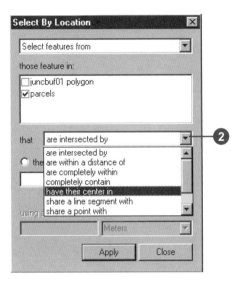

3. Click all to select using all the features.

4. Click the dropdown arrow to choose juncbuf01 polygon. Click Apply.

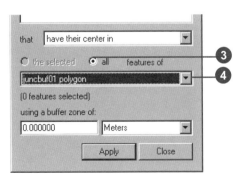

Now the parcels that are within, or mostly within, the 1,000-meter buffer are selected. Click Close.

Increase the suitability code

You can now add to the suitability code for the selected parcels.

1. Right-click the SUITABLE field in the Attributes window. Click Calculate Values.

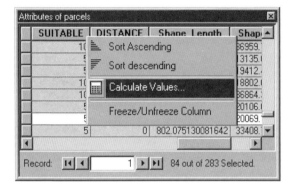

The Field Calculator dialog box appears.

2. Double-click SUITABLE in the Field list.

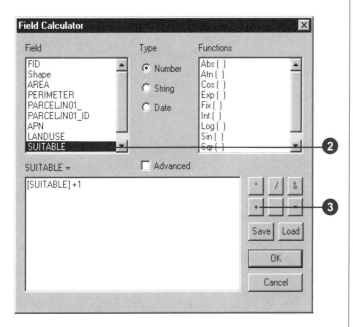

3. Click the plus sign and type "1".

4. Check the expression and then click OK.

The value 1 is added to the suitability codes for the selected features.

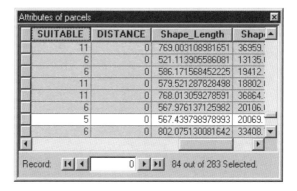

Update the DISTANCE field

While you have these features selected, you can update their DISTANCE fields as well.

1. Click the Attributes button.

Attributes

The Attributes dialog appears.

2. Click parcels at the top of the list of selected features.

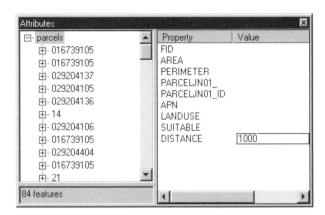

3. Type "1000" in the Value column for the DISTANCE field. Press the Enter key.

Select the closer buffer

Each of the parcels within 1,000 meters of the junction have the value 1000 in their distance field. However, some of these parcels are within 500 meters. You will select the parcels that are closer to the junction and change their distance field.

1. Click Selection and click Select By Attributes.

The Select By Attribute dialog appears.

2. Delete the existing query expression "INSIDE" = 100 AND "FLOODZONE" = 'OUT'.

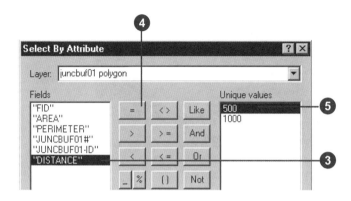

3. Double-click "DISTANCE" in the Fields list.

4. Click the equals button.

5. Double-click 500 in the Unique values list.

6. Verify that the query expression is correct and click OK.

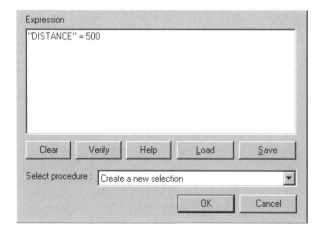

Now the 500-meter buffer is selected.

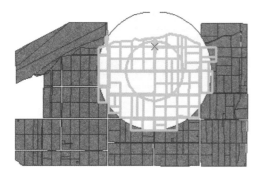

Select the closer parcels

Now that the 500-meter buffer is selected, you can use it to select the parcels that are closer to the junction.

1. Click Selection and click Select By Location.

The Select By Location dialog box appears.

2. Check the box to select parcels.

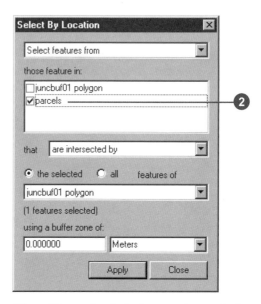

You will use the default selection technique to select parcels that are intersected by the selected features of juncbuf01.

3. Click Apply and click Close.

The parcels that are closest to the junction are now selected.

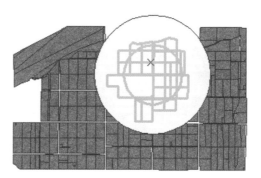

Update the closer parcels

Now you can update the DISTANCE attribute for the selected parcels.

1. Click parcels at the top of the list of selected features.

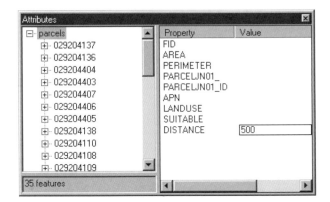

2. Type "500" in the Value column for the DISTANCE field. Press the Enter key.

The DISTANCE attribute is updated in the Attributes window.

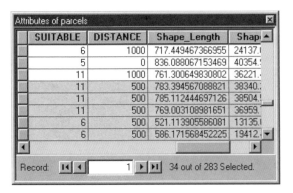

3. Click Editor and click Save Edits.

The changes that you have made to the parcels attributes are saved to the database.

Remove the juncbuf01 layer

Now that you have updated the suitability and distance attributes for these parcels, you can remove juncbuf01 from the map.

1. In the ArcMap table of contents, right-click juncbuf01 polygon. Click Remove.

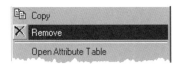

In the next steps, you will find the parcels that are open land.

Selecting a range of values

The land for the new plant should be vacant. In the Assessor's database, vacant land is coded with values ranging from 700 to 799. You will use an attribute query to find values in this range.

Select by attributes

You will use the >= (greater than or equal to) and <= (less than or equal to) operators in this attribute query.

1. Click Selection and click Select By Attributes.

The Select by Attribute dialog box appears. Delete the existing query expression.

2. Double-click [LANDUSE].

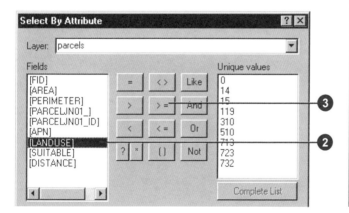

3. Click >= and type "700".

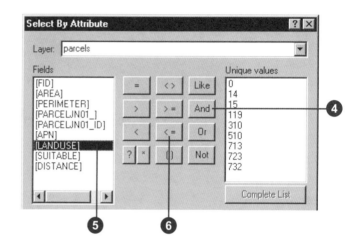

4. Click And.

5. Double-click [LANDUSE].

6. Click <= and type "799".

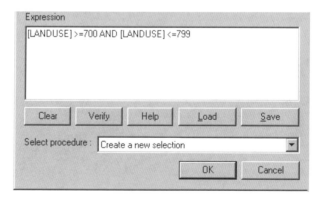

7. Examine the query expression and click OK.

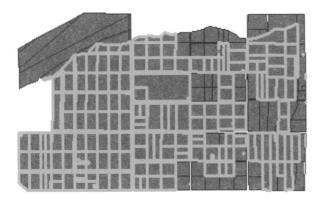

ArcMap selects the parcels that have land use values in the 700s.

Select a feature to remove from the selection

The parcel feature class you created from the Assessor's database does not include the new park. Now you will select the Historic park feature that you added to the park_polygon feature class so that you can remove parcels affected by the development of the park from the selected set of empty parcels.

1. Click and drag parks.lyr from the Catalog onto the map.

2. Click Selection and click Select By Attributes.

3. Click the Layer dropdown arrow and click parks_polygon layer.

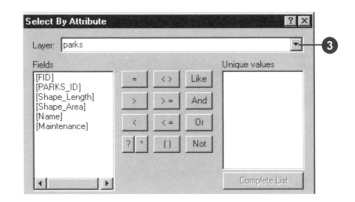

4. Delete the existing query expression.

5. Double-click [Name].

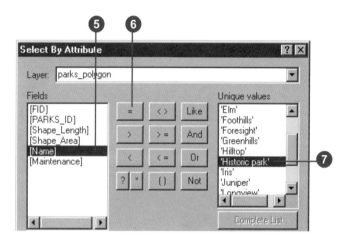

6. Click the equals sign.

7. Double-click 'Historic park'.

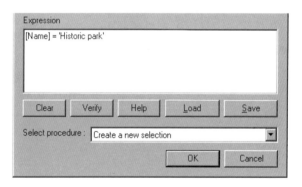

8. Examine the query expression and click OK.

   The park feature is selected.

Remove features from the selection

Now you can remove the parcels that intersect the selected park feature from the set of vacant parcels.

1. Click Selection and click Select By Location.

   The Select By Location dialog box appears.

2. Click the dropdown arrow and click Remove from the current selection of.

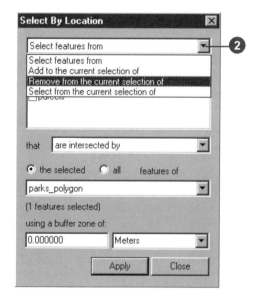

3. Check parcels.

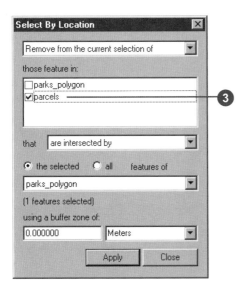

This will remove features from the selected features in the parcels layer that are intersected by the selected features in parks_polygon.

4. Review the information you have entered in the dialog box and click Apply. Click Close.

The parcels that intersect the historic park polygon are removed from the selected set of vacant parcels.

5. Right-click park_polygon in the ArcMap table of contents and click Remove.

Update the suitable field

Now you can add to the suitability code for the selected parcels.

1. Right-click the SUITABLE field in the Attributes window. Click Calculate Values.

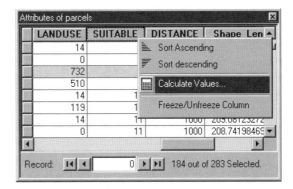

The Field Calculator dialog box appears.

2. Double-click SUITABLE.

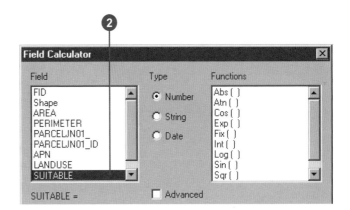

3. Click the plus sign. Type "1". Review the expression and click OK.

The suitability codes of the vacant parcels have now been updated.

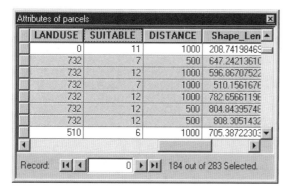

4. Click Editor and click Save Edits.

In the next steps you will find the parcels that are within 50 meters of an existing road.

Selecting with a buffer

The City would prefer that the parcel for the new plant be within 50 meters of an existing road. You will select the streets that are in your project area and use the selected streets to select parcels.

Add the streets

You will use the streets layer to access the data in the GreenvalleyDB geodatabase.

1. Click and drag streets.lyr from the Catalog tree and drop it onto the map.

The streets are drawn on the map.

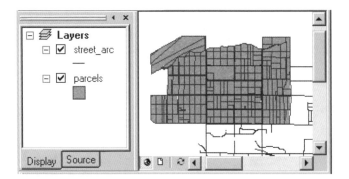

2. Check the box next to parcels in the ArcMap table of contents. This turns off the parcels layer.

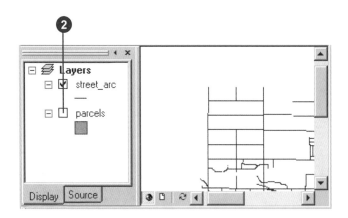

3. Click the Selection button.

You will now select the streets in the project area. After you have selected these streets, you will select the parcels that are intersected by a buffer around them.

4. Click and drag a rectangle around the streets that are visible on the map.

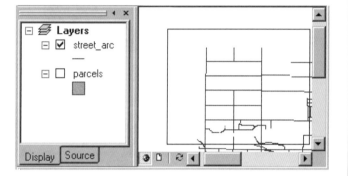

The streets are selected.

5. Check the box to turn the parcels layer back on.

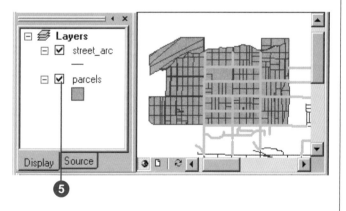

Select parcels with a buffer

Now that you have selected the streets in the project area, you can use them to select parcels that are within 50 meters of a street.

1. Click Select By Location.

2. Type "50" in the text box at the bottom of the Select By Location dialog box to select parcels using a buffer of 50 meters. Accept the default values for the other selection parameters. Click Apply.

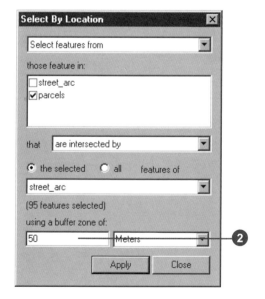

This procedure may take a few minutes.

3. Click Close to close the Select By Location dialog box.

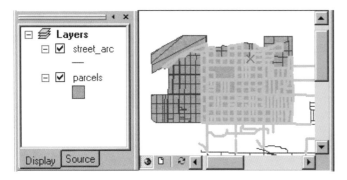

The parcels within 50 meters of existing streets are selected.

Increase the suitability code

Now you can add to the suitability code for the selected parcels.

1. Right-click the SUITABLE field in the Attributes window. Click Calculate Values.

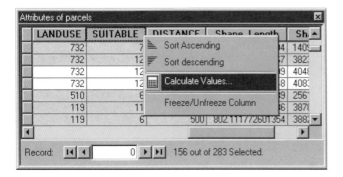

2. Double-click SUITABLE in the Field list.

3. Click the plus sign and type "1".

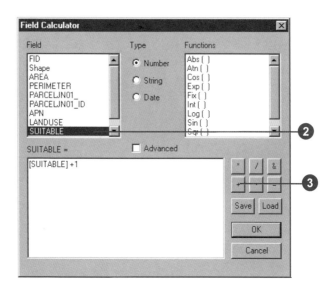

4. Verify the expression and click OK.

5. Click Editor and click Save Edits.

The parcel feature class now contains suitability ranks for all but one of the City's criteria. The parcel selected for the site must be at least 150,000 square meters in area.

Selecting large parcels

The plant site must have an area of at least 150,000 square meters. You will find and investigate the parcels that are this large.

Select by attributes

You will select the parcels by their Shape_Area attribute.

1. Click Selection and click Select By Attributes.

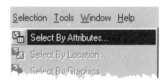

The Select By Attribute dialog box appears.

2. Click the Layer dropdown arrow and click parcels.

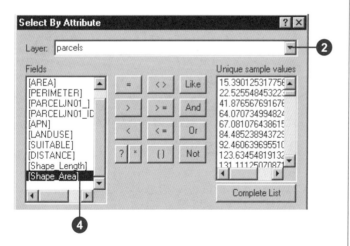

3. Delete the existing query expression.

4. Double-click [Shape_Area].

5. Click the greater than or equal to symbol (>=) and type "150000". Click OK.

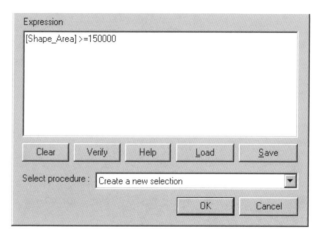

Parcels that are greater than 150,000 square meters are selected.

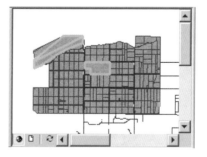

Open the table for the selected features

There are not many parcels bigger than 150,000 square meters. You will examine these parcels more closely.

1. Right-click parcels in the ArcMap table of contents. Click Selection and click Open Table for Selected Features.

The table for the three selected parcels opens.

2. Scroll to the SUITABLE column.

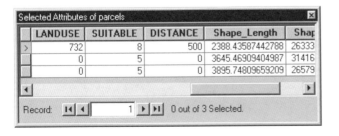

There is a problem. These parcels are large enough to hold the plant, but they all have suitability scores below 10. None of them meets all of the City's required criteria.

3. Close the table.

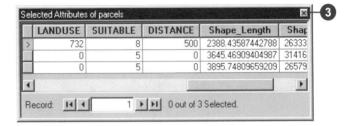

4. Click Selection and click Clear Selected Features.

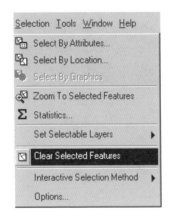

Fortunately, the City is willing to buy more than one adjacent parcel for the plant site.

View the analysis results

Now that you have ranked the parcels, you will change their symbols to show the results of the analysis. You want to be able to see which parcels have suitability values greater than or equal to 10. You also want to be able to differentiate between the suitable parcels based on their suitability values.

Display unique values

You will display the parcels by their suitability rank.

1. Right-click parcels in the ArcMap table of contents and click Properties.

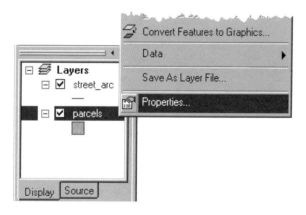

The Properties dialog box appears.

2. Click the Symbology tab.

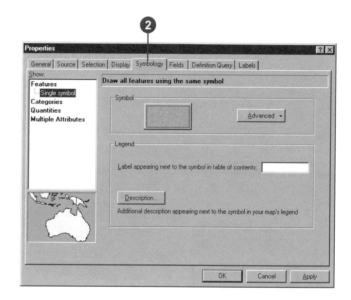

3. Click Categories because you will view the parcel suitability ranks as categorical data.

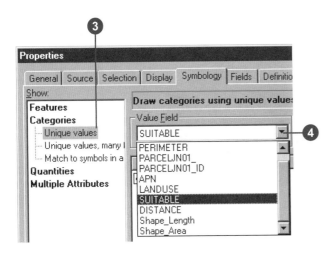

4. Click the Value Field dropdown arrow and click SUITABLE.

5. Click Add Values.

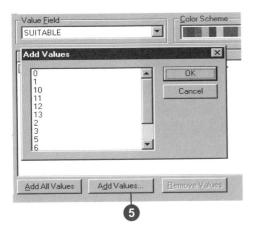

The Add Values dialog box appears.

6. Click 10, press and hold down the Shift key, and click 13. Click OK.

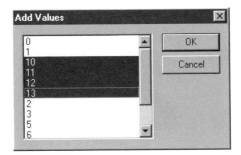

Holding down the Shift key lets you select all values between the two you clicked.

7. Click OK on the Properties dialog box.

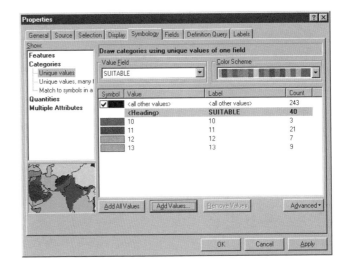

Now you can see the parcels that are not suitable in the "all other values" color and the suitable parcels color-coded according to their suitability.

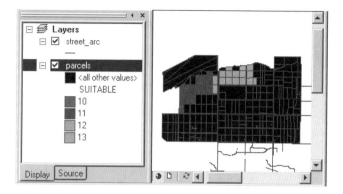

Examine a group of suitable parcels

The City will need to assemble the plant site from a group of suitable parcels. You will check to make sure that enough adjacent parcels are suitable to meet the plant's area requirement of 150,000 meters.

1. Click the Zoom In button.

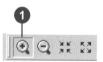

2. Click and drag a rectangle around the group of category 12 and 13 parcels.

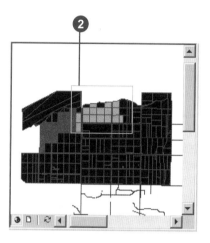

ArcMap zooms to the new extent.

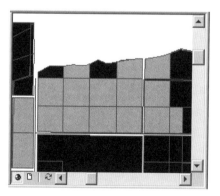

3. Click the Select Features button.

4. Click and drag a box around the intersection of four contiguous suitable parcels.

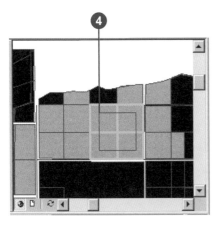

The parcels are selected.

5. Click Selection and click Statistics.

The Selection Statistics dialog box appears.

6. Click the Field dropdown arrow and click Shape_Area.

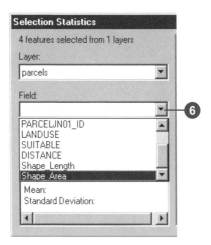

ArcMap calculates summary statistics about the selected parcels and presents a graph of the distribution of values.

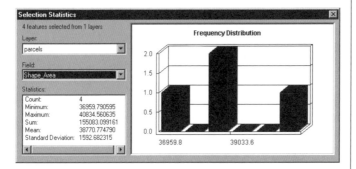

You can see that the sum of the areas of these four selected parcels is 155,083 meters. There is enough room for the plant here. Further examination shows that any four of the eight contiguous parcels in the block of parcels will provide enough room for the plant.

The suitable parcels across the streets to the east and west of this block do not provide enough room for the plant.

7. Close the Selection Statistics dialog box.

8. Click Selection and click Clear Selected Features.

In the next chapter, you will make a map to present the results of your analysis.

Presenting your results

9

IN THIS CHAPTER

- Creating a new layout
- Working with data frames
- Working with layers
- Creating a report
- Adding an extent rectangle
- Adding map elements
- Saving a map
- Exporting an image of a map
- What is next?

In the previous chapter you used a suitability model to rank the parcels according to the City's site selection criteria. You identified the most suitable parcels including a block of eight adjacent parcels that included some of the most suitable parcels. The City will probably choose some combination of four of these parcels.

In this chapter you will create a map to present the results of your analysis. In one data frame you will show all of the suitable parcels symbolized according to their suitability ranks.

In another data frame you will show the highly suitable parcels symbolized according to their rank and their proximity to the main wastewater junction. You will label these parcels with their parcel identification numbers.

In a third data frame you will use an overview map of the City that shows the geographic relationship of the parcels to the rest of the City.

You will create a report showing parcel identification numbers, area, suitability code, and distance from the junction for the highly suitable parcels. You will add this report to the map.

You will add other elements including a North arrow, scale bars, and a title to the map. You will add graphic rectangles to increase the visual appeal of the map.

Finally, you will save the completed map for printing later, and you will export an image of the map for the City to add to the municipal Web site.

Creating a new layout

You will be creating a poster-sized map with three data frames and other map elements. You will work in layout view in order to manage this complex map.

Switch to layout view

First you will switch the map to layout view.

1. Click View and click Layout View.

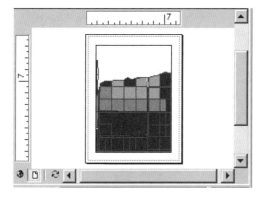

The map switches to layout view.

Change the page size

You will increase the page size to accommodate a larger printed map.

1. Right-click on the page and click Page Setup.

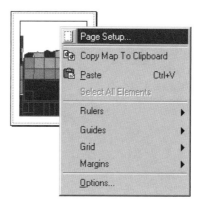

The Page Setup dialog box appears. The Same as Printer box is checked. ArcMap detects the printer's page size.

The City has another printer that is capable of printing D size (22 x 34 inch) pages, so you will set the page size to D.

2. Click the check box to turn off Same as Printer.

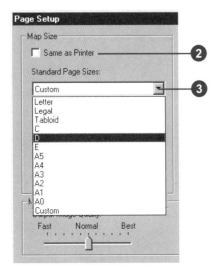

3. Click the Standard Page Sizes dropdown arrow and click D. Now the virtual page for the map will be 22 x 34 inches—D size.

   You want the map poster to be wider than it is high, so change the page orientation.

4. Click Landscape, then click OK on the Page Setup dialog box.

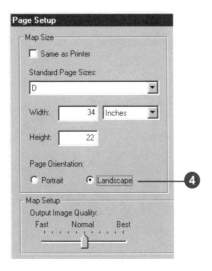

ArcMap adjusts the size and orientation of the virtual page.

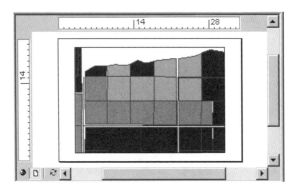

In the next steps you will resize and copy the data frame.

Working with data frames

A data frame is a way of organizing layers together on a map page. In data view you see the contents of a single data frame. In layout view you can work with several data frames on a single map.

The map you are making will have three data frames. It will show the distribution of all of the suitable parcels, the geographic relationship of these parcels to the rest of the City, and some additional information about the most suitable parcels.

Resize the data frame

First you will make this data frame smaller.

1. Click the Select Graphics button.

2. Click near the middle of the data frame.

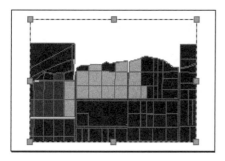

Selection handles appear at the corners of the data frame and along its sides.

3. Move the pointer over the lower-right corner of the data frame. When it turns into the two-pointed resize pointer, click the corner and drag it up and to the left.

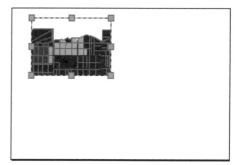

Copy the data frame

Now you will make a copy of the data frame.

1. Click Edit and click Copy.

2. Click Edit and click Paste.

The copy of the data frame is pasted onto the map on top of the original data frame.

3. Click on the data frame and drag the copy below the original.

There are now two data frames on your map.

4. Click Edit and click Paste again.

5. Click on the data frame and drag the copy to the right of the original.

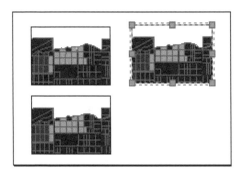

Now there are three data frames on your map.

You will use one of these data frames to show the position of the project area with respect to rest of the City. You will use another to show all of the suitable parcels and their suitability rank. You will use the third data frame to show the most suitable parcels symbolized according to their suitability code and their proximity to the main wastewater junction.

Renaming data frames

The data frames on the map are all titled "Layers". You will give them more descriptive names.

Rename the selected data frame

The data frame that you have just pasted onto the map is still selected—you can see its selection handles in the layout view.

1. Scroll to the bottom of the ArcMap table of contents.

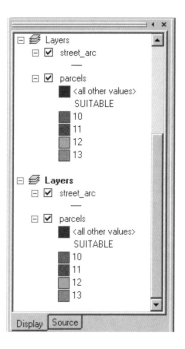

The table of contents is divided into three sections, one for each data frame. Each data frame is titled "Layers".

The last of the three data frames is in bold type—this is the selected data frame.

2. Click the last Layers entry in the table of contents.

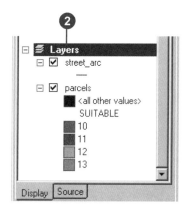

3. Click Layers again.

You can now type a new name for the data frame.

4. Type "City Overview". Press the Enter key.

Rename the other data frames

First you will rename the original data frame.

1. Scroll to the top of the ArcMap table of contents.

2. Click Layers, wait a moment, and then click Layers again.

If you double-click the name of a data frame, you will see the Data Frame Properties dialog box. You do not need to change any properties of the data frame at the moment. If you get this dialog, just click Cancel and try again.

3. Type "Suitable Parcels" and press the Enter key.

4. Scroll to the middle of the ArcMap table of contents.

Now you will rename the other data frame.

5. Click Layers, wait a moment, and then click Layers again.

6. Type "Most Suitable Parcels" and press the Enter key.

You have renamed all of the data frames on the map. In the next step you will change the contents of the City Overview data frame to make it easy for map readers to see the position of the suitable parcels with respect to the rest of Greenvalley.

Customizing the overview data frame

You want the City Overview data frame to show where the suitable parcels are, relative to the rest of Greenvalley. Because most Greenvalley residents are familiar with the major streets of Greenvalley, you can use the streets to show the parcels' location. You will remove the parcels layer from the City Overview data frame, change the extent of the data frame, and change the way the streets are displayed.

Remove a layer in data view

It is often easier to work with the data in a given data frame in data view, particularly when the layout contains several data frames.

1. Click View and click Data View.

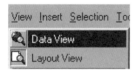

On a map with multiple data frames, switching to data view shows you the data view for the currently selected data frame. In this case, the selected data frame should be City Overview.

2. In the table of contents, right-click on parcels and click Remove.

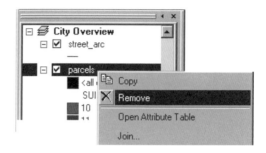

The parcels layer is removed from the map.

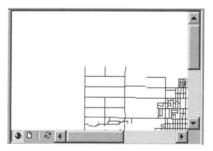

3. Click the Full Extent button.

The map zooms to the full extent of the streets layer.

Change the streets layer properties

This layer shows all of the streets of Greenvalley. Because you did not specify a color scheme, the streets are drawn in a randomly selected color. You will modify two properties of this layer to simplify the representation of the streets.

1. Double-click streets_arc in the table of contents.

Double-clicking a layer is a quick way to get to its Layer Properties dialog.

2. Click the Definition Query tab.

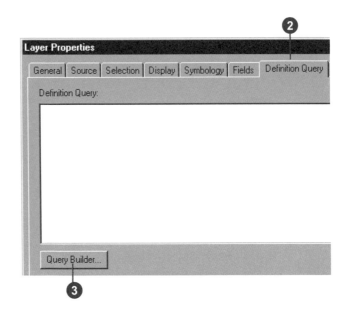

3. Click the Query Builder button on the Definition Query tab.

Show the major streets

The Greenvalley streets in this database belong to three classes. Classes 3 and 4 are major streets; class 5 streets are smaller streets. You will select the major streets.

1. Double-click [Type].

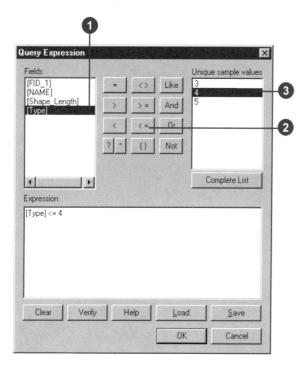

2. Click the less than or equal to button (<=).

3. Double-click 4, review the query expression, and then click OK.

The query expression is added to the Definition Query tab of the Layer Properties dialog box.

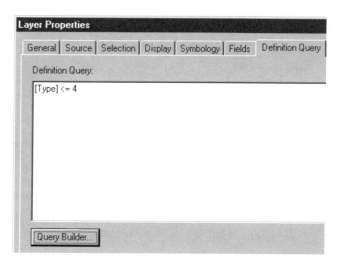

4. Click OK on the Layer Properties dialog.

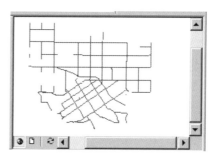

The smaller streets are left off of the map.

Change the street symbol

You want the streets to be drawn with a simple black line.

1. In the table of contents, click the line symbol below the layer name street_arc.

Clicking a symbol in the table of contents is a quick way to get the Symbol Selector dialog box.

2. Click the Major Road symbol and then click OK.

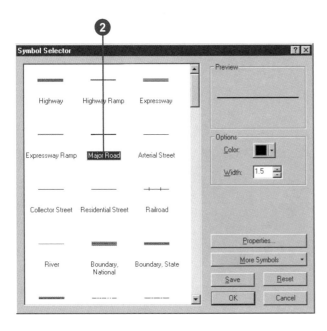

The major streets of Greenvalley are now drawn on the map with a black line.

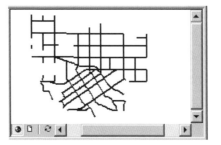

3. Click View and click Layout View.

The City Overview data frame on the map now shows the major streets. In the next step you will make some changes to the Most Suitable Parcels data frame.

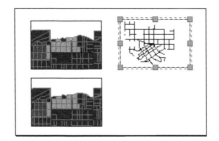

Customizing a second data frame

You will use the Most Suitable Parcels data frame to show a zoomed in view of the best parcels with some additional information.

Remove a layer in layout view

Sometimes it is convenient to work with the layers in a data frame while still in Layout View.

1. Scroll the table of contents to the Most Suitable Parcels data frame.

2. Right-click street_arc and click Remove.

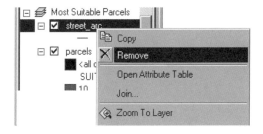

The Most Suitable Parcels data frame now only contains the parcels layer.

Change the symbology of the parcels layer

You will use the parcels layer as a background layer to show the parcel boundaries. The foreground data in this data frame will be a new layer containing the most suitable parcels.

1. Right-click parcels in the Most Suitable Parcels data frame in the table of contents.

The layer Properties dialog box appears.

2. Click the Symbology tab.

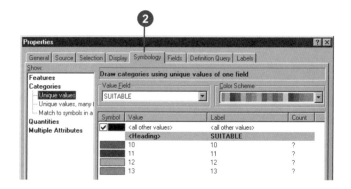

3. Click Features. Click OK.

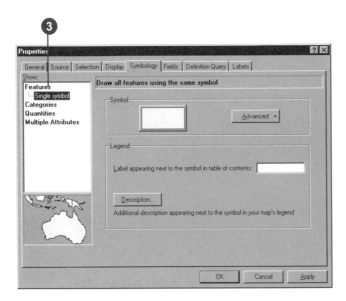

The parcels are drawn with a single color fill symbol. This color is randomly selected and is probably not the shade of gray that you planned for the parcels layer.

4. In the table of contents, right-click on the new color patch for the parcels layer. Click a light gray.

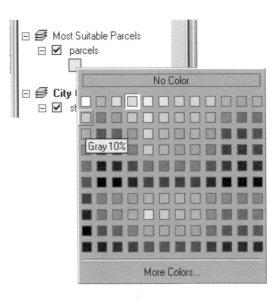

Right-clicking a symbol in the table of contents is a shortcut to the symbol color palette. Left-clicking a symbol is a shortcut to the Symbol Selector dialog box.

Now you have prepared the background data layer for this data frame. In the next step you will create a new layer of the most suitable parcels.

Creating a selection layer

You will use the parcels layer in the Most Suitable Parcels data frame to create a new layer. This new layer will show the most suitable of the parcels. You will use a Select By Attribute query to find these parcels.

Select the correct data frame

In Layout view, queries are performed on the selected data frame. You have been making changes to the layers in the Most Suitable Parcels data frame, but it is not the selected data frame (City Overview is selected). Before you can query the parcels layer you must select the Most Suitable Parcels data frame.

1. Click the Most Suitable Parcels data frame on the virtual page.

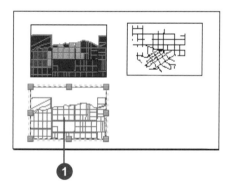

The data frame is now selected.

Select the most suitable parcels

You can now query the parcels layer to find the most suitable parcels, those with suitability codes of 12 or 13.

1. Click Selection and click Select By Attributes.

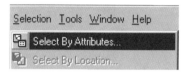

The Select By Attribute dialog box appears.

2. Delete the previous query, then double-click SUITABLE.

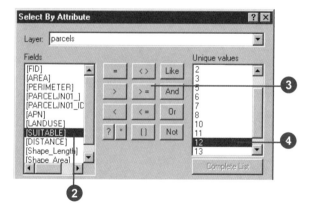

3. Click the greater than or equal to button (>=).

4. Double-click 12.

5. Verify that the selection expression is correct and then click OK.

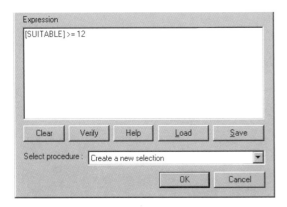

Now the most suitable parcels are selected.

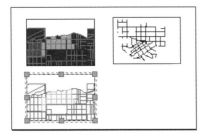

Create a new layer of the selected parcels

The most suitable parcels are selected. You will create a new layer of these selected features.

1. Right-click parcels in the table of contents, point to Selection, and point to Create Layer From Selected Features.

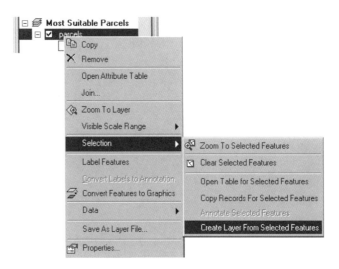

ArcMap creates a new layer that contains the selected features.

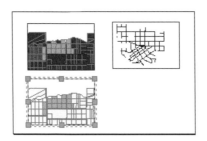

2. Click parcels selection in the table of contents.

3. Click parcels selection again to edit the layer name.
4. Type "Best Candidates" and press the Enter key.

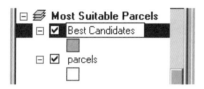

The layer is renamed in the table of contents. Now you will change the way it is symbolized and add the parcel identification numbers as labels on the map.

Symbolizing the new layer

Some of the Best Candidates parcels have higher suitability scores than others—those within 50 meters of a road have a score of 13, the others have a score of 12—and some are closer to the junction where the plant will be joined to the existing wastewater system. These differences may play a part in the City Council's decision of which parcels to buy for the plant site. You will symbolize the layer so that both pieces of information are communicated.

Show unique values from multiple fields

Now you will change the layer's symbology.

1. Double-click Best Candidates in the table of contents.

Double-clicking a layer name is a shortcut to the layer properties—the Layer Properties dialog box appears.

2. Click the Symbology tab, then click Categories.

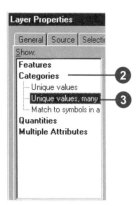

3. Click Unique values, many fields.

Now you will specify the two fields on which ArcMap will symbolize this layer.

4. Click the first dropdown arrow in the Value Fields section and click SUITABLE.

5. Click the second dropdown arrow in the Value Fields section and click DISTANCE.

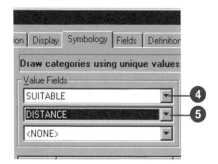

Now add the values to include on the map.

6. Click Add Values. The Add Values dialog appears.

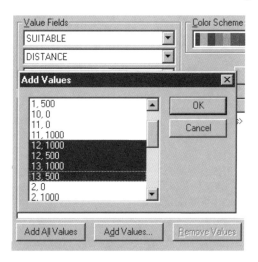

7. Click 12, 1000 and then hold the Shift key down and click 13, 500. These values and the two pairs of values between them are selected. Click OK.

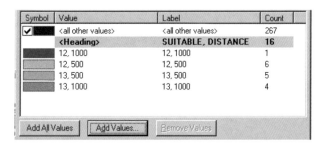

The four pairs of values will be shown on the map with unique symbols.

Change the field labels

Now you will change the labels that appear in the table of contents and the legend to make them easier to understand.

1. Click the label field for 12, 1000 and type "Very Suitable, Far".

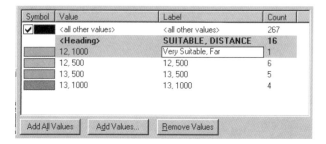

2. Change the labels for the remaining three symbols.

For 12, 500 type "Very Suitable, Near".

For 13, 500 type "Most Suitable, Near".

For 13, 1000 type "Most Suitable, Far".

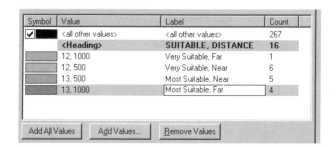

3. Uncheck the box for all other values. Click OK.

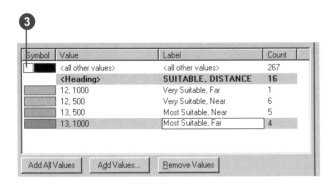

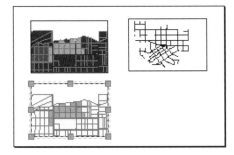

The layer now has symbols that show unique combinations of the two fields.

Change the extent of the data frame

You want the Most Suitable Parcels data frame to emphasize these parcels, so you will zoom in close to them.

1. Click the Zoom In button.

2. Click and drag a rectangle around the Best Candidate parcels.

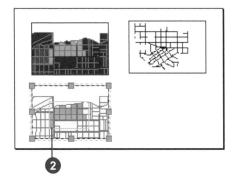

The parcels of interest now occupy more of the data frame.

Labeling the new layer

You will add the parcels' identification numbers to the map as labels, so the council can look up parcels from this layer in a table that you will provide. The parcel numbers are stored in the APN field.

Set the label field

Before you add the labels you will make sure that the correct field is used.

1. Double-click Best Candidates.

2. Click the Labels tab of the Layer Properties dialog box.

3. Click the dropdown arrow to select the label field and click APN.

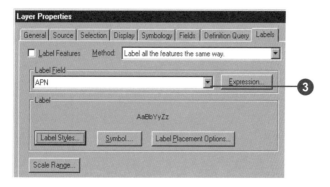

Set the font size

You will use an 18 point font to label the parcels.

1. Click Symbol. The Symbol Selector dialog box appears.

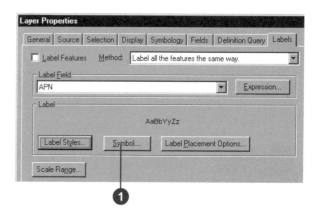

2. Type "18" in the Size box. Click OK.

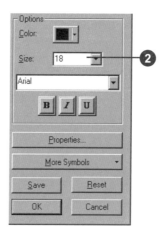

3. Click OK on the Layer Properties dialog box.

Label the parcels

You can now label the parcels.

1. Right-click Best Candidates and click Label Features.

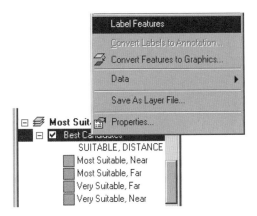

ArcMap adds the parcel numbers to the features in the Best Candidates layer.

Now the Best Candidates parcels have unique symbols and labels. You will create a report on these parcels, add it to the map, and then finish laying out the map.

Creating a report

You will create a tabular report of the suitability code, distance from the junction, area, and parcel identification number for each of the Best Candidate parcels.

Start the Report tool

First you will start the Make Report tool.

1. Click Tools and click Make Report.

The Report Properties dialog appears.

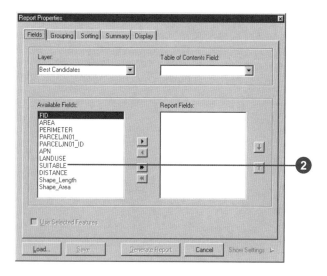

2. Double-click SUITABLE to move it from the Available Fields to the Report Fields column.

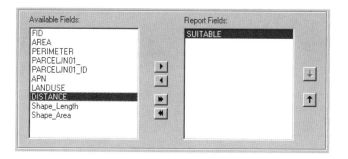

3. Double-click DISTANCE, Shape_Length, and APN.

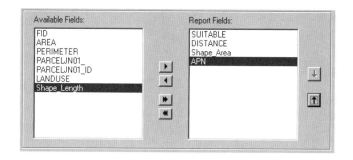

Group records in the report

Now you will group the records according to their suitability code.

1. Click the Grouping tab.

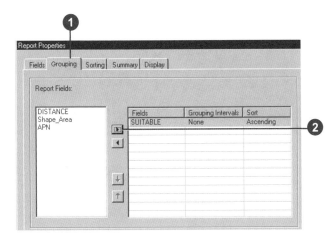

2. Click the upper arrow button to use the SUITABLE field for grouping.

Sort records in the report

You will sort the records in each group according to their DISTANCE code.

1. Click the Sorting tab.

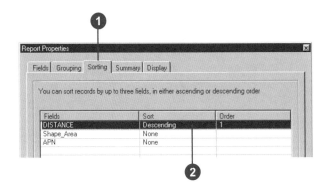

2. Click in the Sorting column for DISTANCE and click Descending.

Generate the report

Now you will have ArcMap generate the report using the settings you have specified.

1. Click Generate Report.

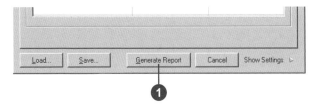

The Report Viewer appears.

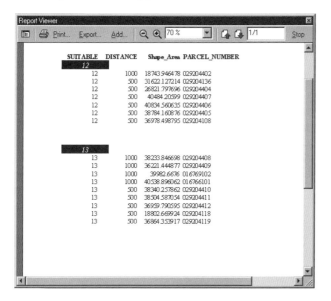

You want to add this report to the map.

2. Click Add.

The Add to Map dialog box appears. The report is only one page long, so you will accept the default setting.

3. Click OK.

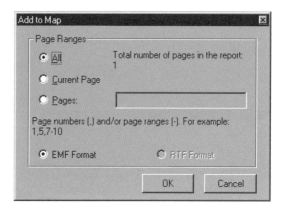

The report is added to the map.

4. Click the x button to close the Report Viewer.

5. Click the Close button to close the Report Properties dialog box.

The Report Tool asks if you want to save this report.

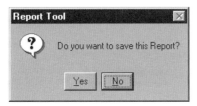

6. Click No.

   The report appears on the virtual page.

7. Click and drag the report into position beside the Most Suitable Parcels data frame.

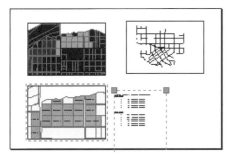

Adding an extent rectangle

You will add a rectangle to the City Overview data frame that will show the location of the suitable parcels relative to the rest of the City. Extent rectangles show the size, shape, and position of one data frame in another data frame.

Select the City Overview

First you will need to select the City Overview data frame.

1. Click the Select Graphics button.

2. Click the City Overview data frame to select it.

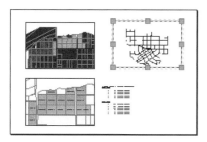

3. Right-click on the data frame and click Properties.

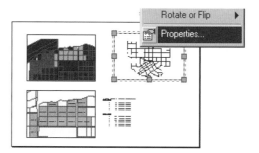

The City Overview Properties dialog box appears.

4. Click the Extent Rectangles tab.

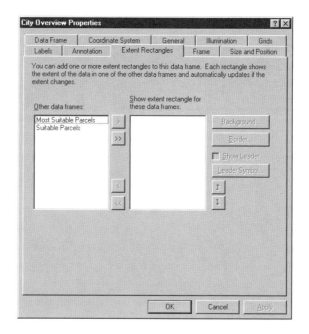

Select a data frame

You will show the position of the Suitable Parcels data frame.

1. Click Suitable Parcels in the Other data frames list.

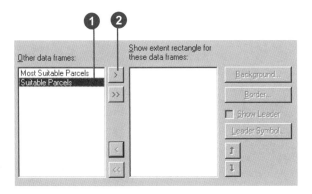

2. Click the top arrow button to move Suitable Parcels to the other list.

   The Background and Border buttons become active when you add Suitable Parcels to the list.

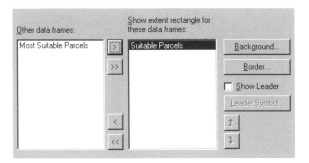

Select a border

You add a border to the extent rectangle to show the location of the suitable parcels relative to the streets.

1. Click Border.

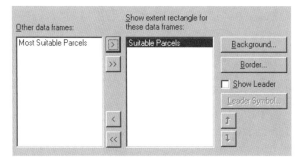

The Border Selector appears.

2. Click the 2.0 Point border. Click OK.

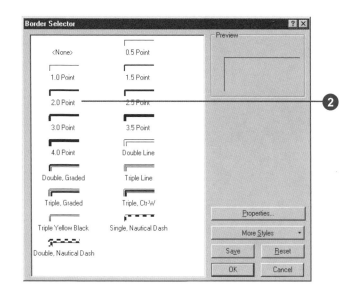

3. Click OK on the City Overview Properties dialog box.

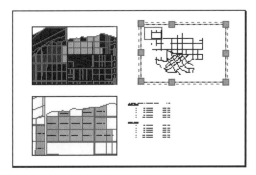

The extent rectangle appears in the City Overview data
frame. It shows the position and extent of the Suitable
Parcels data frame.

Map readers will now be able to see the location of the
suitable parcels relative to the major streets of Greenvalley.

Adding legends

Two data frames, Suitable Parcels and Most Suitable Parcels, show the parcels symbolized in different ways. You will add two legends to this map, one for each of these data frames.

Add a legend for Suitable Parcels

First you will need to select the Suitable Parcels data frame.

1. Click the Select Graphics button.

2. Click the Suitable Parcels data frame.

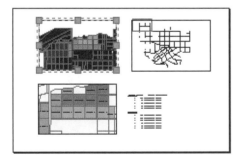

Now the data frame is selected and you can add a legend for it.

3. Click Insert and click Legend.

The legend appears near the middle of the map.

4. Click the legend and drag it to the lower-right side of the virtual page.

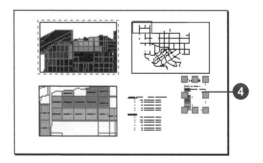

Now you will add another legend for the Most Suitable Parcels data frame.

Add a legend for Most Suitable Parcels

First you will need to select the Suitable Parcels data frame.

1. Click the Most Suitable Parcels data frame.

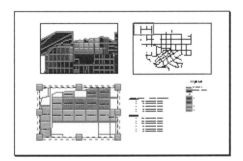

The data frame is selected.

2. Click Insert and click Legend.

The legend is inserted.

3. Click the legend and drag it below the first legend.

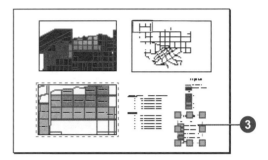

Now both of the data frames have legends. To make the map more attractive, you will remove the title "legend" from the Most Suitable Parcels legend.

Change legend properties

You will change one of the legend's properties to remove its title. Because you have just added it, the Most Suitable Parcels legend is selected.

1. Right-click on the Most Suitable Parcels legend and click Properties.

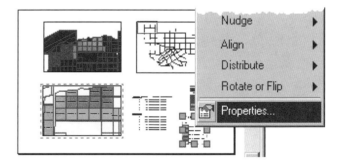

The Legend Properties dialog box appears.

2. Click the Show check box to remove the check mark.

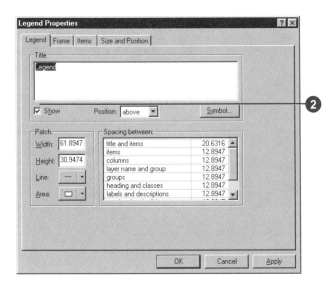

The Title box becomes grayed out.

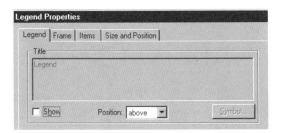

3. Click OK.

Now the legend does not have a title.

Align the two legends

You want the two legends to be neatly aligned with each other. You will zoom in to the layout and align the legends.

1. Click the Zoom In tool on the Layout toolbar.

This tool lets you zoom in to the virtual page so you can examine and work with the map elements on the page.

2. Click on the page and drag a rectangle around the two legends.

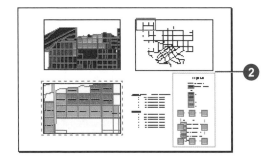

ArcMap zooms in to show this area of the page in more detail.

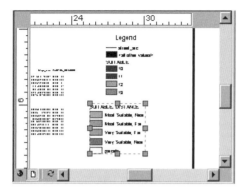

3. Click the Select Graphics button.

4. Hold the Shift key and click the upper legend patch to select it.

Holding the Shift key while you click allows you to select multiple objects on the layout.

5. Right-click on the upper legend patch, click Align, and click Align Left.

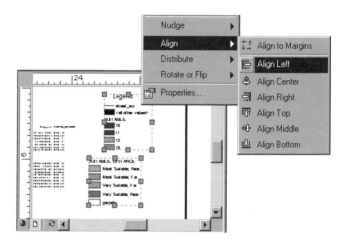

The patches are aligned with one another.

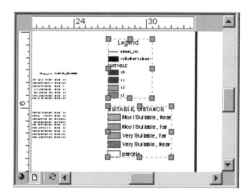

Group the two legends

You will be rearranging the elements on the page. To keep the two legend patches together when you do so, you will group them.

1. Right-click on the upper legend patch and click Group.

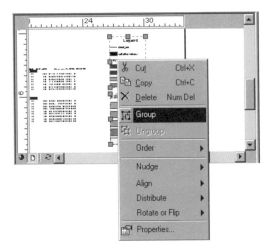

The two legend patches are now grouped together. You can move them as a single graphic object.

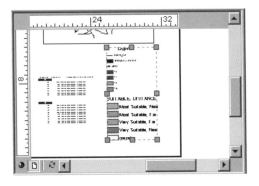

2. Click the Zoom Whole Page button on the Layout toolbar.

The map zooms to fit the ArcMap window.

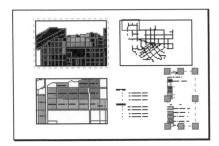

Now you are ready to add a few final map elements to finish the map. You will include a North arrow, scale bars for each data frame, and a title. You will also add two graphic rectangles to tie the composition together.

Adding a North arrow

To finish this map, you will add a title, North arrow, scale bars for each data frame, and graphic rectangles to tie the composition together.

Add a North arrow

You will place a North arrow to show the orientation of the whole map.

1. Click the Select Graphics button.

2. Click Insert and click North Arrow.

The North Arrow Selector dialog box appears.

3. Click a North arrow. Click OK.

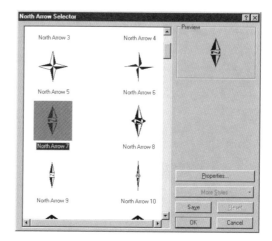

The North arrow appears on the map.

4. Click the North arrow and drag it to the upper-left corner of the map.

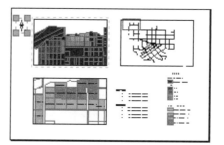

The map now has a North arrow.

Adding scale bars

This map has three data frames, each with a different scale. You will add a scale bar for each data frame.

Add a scale bar

You will place a scale bar below each data frame. You will start with the City Overview data frame.

1. Click the City Overview data frame to select it.

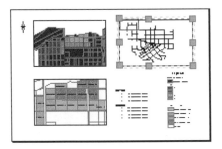

2. Click Insert and click Scale Bar.

The Scale Bar Selector dialog box appears.

3. Click a scale bar and click OK.

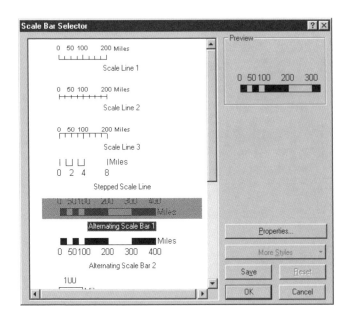

The scale bar is added to the map.

4. Click the scale bar and drag it below the City Overview data frame.

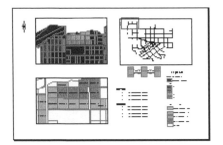

Add a second scale bar

Now you will add a scale bar for the Suitable Parcels data frame.

1. Click the Suitable Parcels data frame to select it.

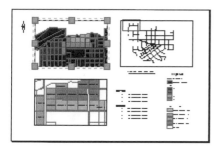

2. Click Insert and click Scale Bar.

The Scale Bar Selector dialog box appears.

3. Click a scale bar and click OK.

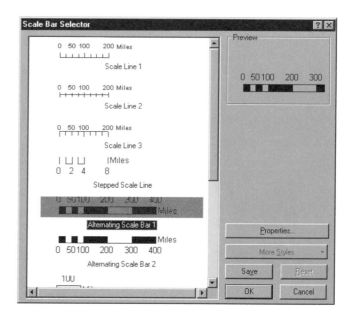

The scale bar appears on the map.

4. Click the scale bar and drag it below the Suitable Parcels data frame.

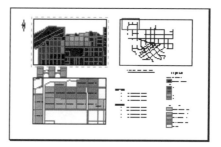

Now you will add a third scale bar for the third data frame.

Add a third scale bar

Now you will add a scale bar for the Most Suitable Parcels data frame.

1. Click the Most Suitable Parcels data frame to select it.

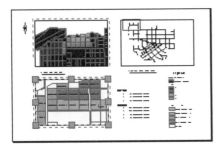

You will simply repeat the procedure you used to insert the second scale bar.

2. Click Insert and click Scale Bar.

3. Click a scale bar and click OK.

4. Click the scale bar and drag it below the Most Suitable Parcels data frame.

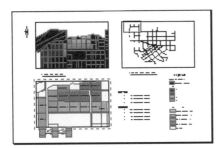

Now you have added scale bars for each of the data frames.

Adding a title

Add a title

You will add a descriptive title to the map.

1. Click Insert and click Title.

The text "Enter Map Title" appears on the map.

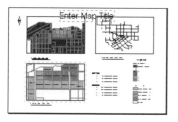

2. Type "Potential Plant Sites".

3. On the Drawing toolbar, type "72" in the font size text box and press the Enter key.

The map title appears in 72-point type.

Rotate the title

You will rotate the title and place it along the left edge of the map.

1. Right-click on the title, click Rotate or Flip, and click Rotate Left.

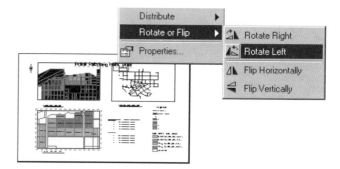

The title is rotated. Now you can place it along the left edge of the map.

2. Click on the title and drag it to the left edge of the map below the North arrow.

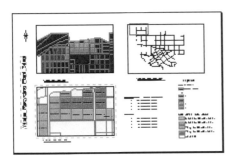

You have added the map elements that you wanted to the map and arranged them on the page. Now you will add the graphic rectangles.

Adding graphic rectangles

You will use two graphic rectangles to make your map look more polished. The first will frame the title and North arrow, and the second will tie the entire composition together.

Add a rectangle

You will place one graphic rectangle behind the title and North arrow.

1. Click the Rectangle button on the Drawing toolbar.

2. Click below and to the left of the title and drag a rectangle around the title and the North arrow.

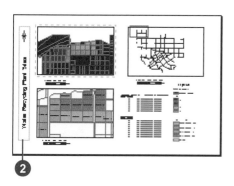

The graphic rectangle appears on the map.

3. Right-click the rectangle, click Order, and click Send to Back.

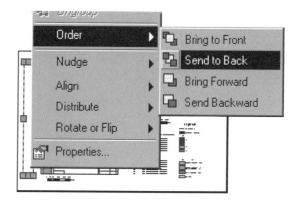

The rectangle is now behind the title and North arrow.

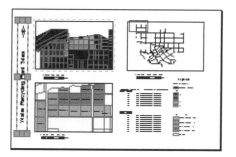

4. Click the dropdown arrow beside the Fill button on the Drawing toolbar.

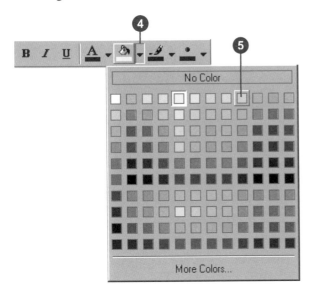

5. Click a light blue from the color menu.

The rectangle is drawn in light blue.

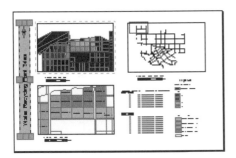

You have framed the title and North arrow. Now you will frame the map composition.

Add a second rectangle

You will place the second graphic rectangle behind all of the elements on the page to frame the map.

1. Click the Rectangle button on the Drawing toolbar.

2. Click at the upper-left corner of the map and drag a rectangle to the lower-right corner of the map.

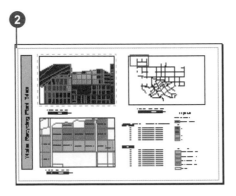

The second graphic rectangle appears on the map.

3. Right-click the rectangle, click Order, and click Send to Back.

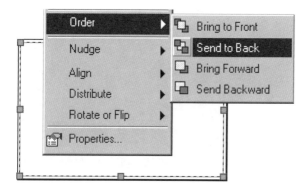

The rectangle is drawn behind the other page elements.

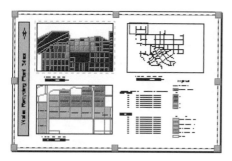

You have completed the poster map for the City Council meeting.

When you produce maps for publication, it is a good idea to check the final map for errors. This should include proofreading text, reviewing the symbology to make sure it is clear, and reviewing the map composition for balance. You should print the map to verify the colors—this will also make it easier to do other proofreading work.

Saving the map

Now that you have finished laying out the map, you will save it.

1. Click File and click Save As.

The Save As dialog box appears.

2. Navigate to the maps folder in the project folder.

3. Type "Greenvalley Treatment Plant Sites" and click Save.

Later, when you need to print or view this map again, it will be available, exactly as you have created it.

Exporting an image of the map

Now that you have saved a copy of the map that you can print later, you will make a few changes and export a page-sized JPEG image of the map for the City's Web site.

Because the JPEG image of the map will be displayed on computer screens over the Web, you will readjust the page size of the map.

As a result of this change you will also have to change the font size of the labels in the Most Suitable Parcels data frame.

Change the page size

1. Click File and click Page Setup.

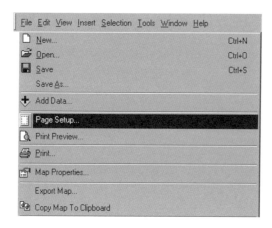

The Page Setup dialog box appears.

The page size is set to "D". You will change it to letter size.

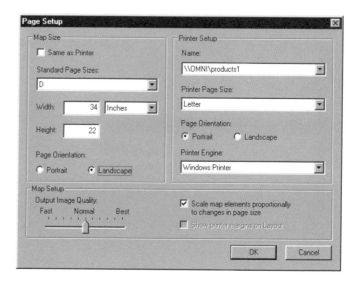

2. Click the dropdown arrow under Standard Page Sizes and click Letter to reset the page size. Click OK.

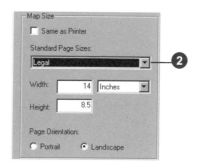

The map rescales to page size. This will fit better on a computer screen.

Export the map

1. Click File and click Export Map.

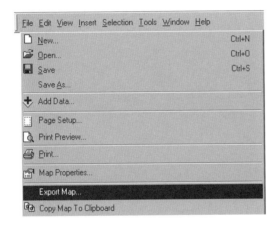

The Export dialog box appears.

2. Navigate to the maps folder in the project folder.

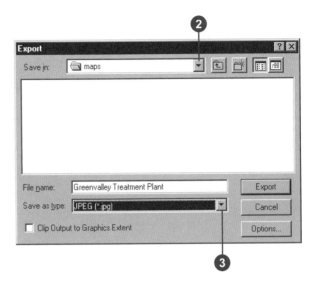

3. Click the dropdown arrow to choose the file type. Click JPEG [*.jpg].

4. Type "Greenvalley Treatment Plant" in the File name text box and click Export.

   ArcMap creates a JPEG image of the map.

Now you can give the City's Web master the image for the municipal Web site.

What's next?

You have finished the GIS analysis project. If you have a question about how to perform a specific task with desktop ArcInfo applications, you can look up the task in the *Using ArcMap*, *Using ArcCatalog*, or *Using ArcToolbox* reference books. If you want to learn how to create geodatabases, read *Building a Geodatabase*. You can also find answers in the online help.

If you are interested in learning about GIS data models and how ArcInfo implements the geodatabase data model, or if you are interested in learning specifics about how to develop applications with ArcInfo, you should read *Modeling Our World* and the *ArcObjects Developer's Guide*.

Glossary

active data frame

The data frame that is currently being worked on, for example, layers are being added. The active data frame is shown in bold text in the table of contents.

address geocoding

The process of assigning x,y coordinates to addresses so that they can be displayed as points on a map.

AML

ARC Macro Language. A high-level algorithmic language for generating end-user applications. Features include the ability to create on-screen menus, use and assign variables, control statement execution, and get and use map or page unit coordinates.

AML includes an extensive set of commands that can be used interactively or in AML programs (macros), as well as commands that report on the status of ArcInfo environment settings.

analysis

The process of identifying a question or issue to be addressed, modeling the issue, investigating model results, interpreting the results, and possibly making a recommendation. See model and spatial analysis.

arc–node topology

Arcs represent linear features and the borders of area features. Every arc has a from-node, which is the first vertex in the arc, and a to-node, which is the last vertex. Nodes indicate the endpoints and intersections of arcs. They do not exist as independent features. Together they define the direction of the arc. Arc-node topology defines connectivity in coverages—arcs are connected to each other if they share a common node.

ArcPress

ArcPress is a raster printing extension for ArcInfo. ArcPress allows you to easily print ArcInfo maps on a variety of supported raster printers or convert them to a bitmap format for interchange in other graphics applications.

ArcSDE

ArcSDE is an application server and open data manager. ArcSDE is the standard interface that allows ESRI GIS software direct access to spatial features that are stored and managed in a relational or object-relational database management system.

aspatial query

See attribute query and query.

attribute

1. A piece of information describing a map feature. The attributes of a ZIP Code, for example, might include its area, population, and average per capita income.

2. A characteristic of a geographic feature described by numbers, characters, images, and CAD drawings, typically stored in tabular format and linked to the feature by a user-assigned identifier. For example, the attributes of a well might include depth and gallons per minute.

A column in a database table. See also item.

attribute query

A query of attributes in a table or feature class. Also called aspatial query. See also query.

attribute table

An INFO or other tabular file containing rows and columns. In ArcInfo, attribute tables are associated with a class of geographic features such as wells or roads. Each row represents a geographic feature. Each column represents one attribute of a feature, with the same column representing the same attribute in each row. See also feature attribute table.

backup

A copy of a file, a set of files, or a whole disk for safekeeping in case the original is lost or damaged.

batch mode operation

Executes a given ArcToolbox tool two or more times. It includes a utility to save the batch entries as a geoprocessing AML and reload the AML for later execution.

Boolean expression

A type of expression that reduces to a true or false (logical) condition. A Boolean expression contains logical expressions (for example, DEPTH > 100) and Boolean operators. A Boolean operator is a keyword that specifies how to combine simple logical expressions into complex expressions. Boolean operators negate a predicate (NOT), specify a combination of predicates (AND), or specify a list of alternative predicates (OR). For example, DEPTH > 100 AND DIAMETER > 20.

buffer

A zone of a specified distance around coverage features. Both constant- and variable-width buffers can be generated by ArcToolbox for a set of coverage features based on each feature's attribute values. The resulting buffer zones form polygons (areas) that are either inside or outside the specified buffer distance from each feature. Buffers are useful for proximity analysis (for example, find all stream segments within 300 feet of a proposed logging area). ArcMap can create feature buffers and graphics.

complex edge feature

A linear network feature that can support one or more junctions along its length, yet remain a single feature. See simple edge feature.

complex junction feature

A linear network feature that can contain internal parts that play a logical and topological role in a network. For example, the state of the junction determines whether features can be connected or disconnected. See simple junction feature.

connection

See folder connection.

connectivity

The topological identification of connected arcs by recording the from- and to-node for each arc. Arcs that share a common node are connected. See also arc–node topology.

contiguity

The topological identification of adjacent polygons by recording the left and right polygons of each arc. See also polygon–arc topology.

coordinate system

A reference system used to measure horizontal and vertical distances on a planimetric map. A coordinate system is usually defined by a map projection, a spheroid of reference, a datum, one or more standard parallels, a central meridian, and possible shifts in the x- and y-directions to locate x,y positions of point, line, and area features.

In ArcInfo, a system with units and characteristics defined by a map projection. A common coordinate system is used to spatially register geographic data for the same area.

coverage

A vector data storage format for storing the location, shape, and attributes of geographic features. One of the primary vector data storage formats for ArcInfo.

custom behavior

Behavior is the implementation of an object class method. ESRI-provided objects have a set of methods associated with them. A developer can choose to override one of these methods or create additional methods. In this instance, the object is said to have custom behavior.

custom feature

A feature with specialized behavior instantiated in a class by a developer.

data frame

A frame on the map that displays layers occupying the same geographic area. You may have one or more data frames on your map depending upon how you want to organize your data. For instance, one data frame might highlight a study area and another might provide an overview of where the study area is.

data model

See georelational data model and geodatabase data model.

data view

An all-purpose view for exploring, displaying, and querying geographic data. This view hides all map elements such as titles, North arrows, and scale bars. See also layout view.

database connection

A connection in ArcCatalog to an SDE or OLE DB database.

digitize

To enter vector feature data into a GIS from hardcopy maps or images on screen.

element

See map element.

erase

An ArcInfo command that erases the input coverage features that overlap the erase coverage polygons.

extent rectangle

A rectangle that is displayed in one data frame, showing the size and position of another data frame.

extract wizard

An ArcToolbox wizard that selects features from a coverage based on attribute values and creates a new coverage.

feature

A representation of a real-world object.

feature attribute table

A table used to store attribute information for a specific feature class.

feature class

A group of features with the same geometry and attribute fields.

A feature class may be stored with other feature classes in a feature dataset in a geodatabase, or as a standalone feature class in a geodatabase, or in a shapefile, or with other feature classes of a different geometry in a coverage.

feature dataset

A collection of feature classes that share the same spatial reference. Because the feature classes share the same spatial reference, they can participate in topological relationships with each other such as in a geometric network. Several feature classes with the same geometry may be stored in the same feature dataset. Object classes and relationship classes can also be stored in a feature dataset.

folder connection

A top-level branch of the Catalog tree that provides quick access to a location in the file system. You can make connections to hard drives, folders, and geodatabases.

geodatabase data model

Geographic data model that represents geographic features as objects in an object-relational database. Features are stored as rows in a table; geometry is stored in a shape field. Supports sophisticated modeling of real-world features. Objects may have custom behavior.

geoprocessing

GIS operations such as geographic feature overlay, coverage selection and analysis, topology processing, and data conversion.

georelational data model

Geographic data model that represents geographic features as an interrelated set of spatial and descriptive data. The Georelational model is the fundamental data model used by the previous versions of ArcInfo.

GIS

Geographic information system. An organized collection of computer hardware, software, geographic data, and personnel designed to efficiently capture, store, update, manipulate, analyze, and display all forms of geographically referenced information.

A GIS may be used for a project (also called project GIS, or single-user GIS), by a department of an organization to support a key function of that department (called departmental GIS), or by an organization to support daily activities and strategic decision making (called enterprise GIS).

grid

A geographic representation of the world as an array of equally sized square cells arranged in rows and columns. Each grid cell is referenced by its geographic x,y location. See raster.

identity

The topological overlay of a coverage (input) with a polygon coverage (identity). For each feature in the input coverage, the intersection with identity features is determined, creating new features of the same feature class as the input coverage. For example, a road (input coverage, arc feature class) passing through two counties (identity coverage) would be split into two arc features, each with the attributes of the road and the county it passes through. Compare with intersect and union.

image

Represents geographic features by dividing the world into discrete squares called cells. Examples include satellite and aerial photographs, scanned documents, and building photographs. See also raster.

intersect

The topological integration of two spatial datasets that preserves features that fall within the area common to both input datasets. See also identity and union.

item

A column of information in an attribute table, for example, a single attribute of a record in an INFO data file.

label

Text on a map that provides map readers with additional information about a feature. ArcMap can label features on the fly with any of their attributes (or with text from several fields) and has advanced options for label placement and visibility. Labels can be made into annotation layers and then stored in geodatabases.

layer

A collection of similar geographic features—such as rivers, lakes, counties, or cities—of a particular area or place for display on a map. A layer references geographic data stored in a data source, such as a coverage, and defines how to display it.

layout view

The view for laying out your map. Layout view shows the virtual page upon which you place and arrange geographic data and map elements—such as titles, legends, and scale bars—for printing. See also data view.

left–right topology

The topological data structure ArcInfo uses to represent contiguity between polygons. Left–right topology supports analysis functions such as adjacency. See also topology.

legend

A list of symbols appearing on the map; includes a sample of each symbol and text describing what feature each symbol represents.

location query

Also called spatial query. Selection of features by their geometric relationship with other features. See also query.

map

1. A graphical presentation of geographic information. It contains geographic data and other elements such as a title, North arrow, legend, and scale bar. You can interactively display and query the geographic data on a map and also prepare a

printable map by arranging the map elements around the data in a visually pleasing manner.

2. A map is a document that lets you display and work with geographic data. A map contains one or more layers of geographic data and various supporting map elements such as scale bars. Layers on a map are contained in data frames. A data frame has properties such as scale, projection and extent, and also graphic properties such as where it is located on your map's page. Some maps have one data frame, while other more advanced maps may have several data frames.

map element

A graphic component, such as a scale bar, North arrow, and title, that helps describe the geographic data on the map.

metadata

Information about GIS data that allows someone to determine if the GIS data is suitable for a particular purpose. ArcCatalog stores metadata in XML (extensible markup language), so the same metadata can be viewed in many different ways using different style sheets.

model

1. An abstraction of reality.

2. A set of clearly defined analytical procedures used to derive new information.

3. A data representation of reality (for example, vector data model, TIN data model, raster data model).

North arrow

A map component that shows how a map is oriented.

Overlay wizard

An ArcToolbox wizard that uses overlay operations to create a new coverage by computing the geometric intersection of two coverages–an input coverage and an overlay coverage.

See also identity, intersect, and union.

Pan

To move the viewing window up, down, or sideways to display areas in a geographic dataset that, at the current viewing scale, lies outside the viewing window. See also zoom.

Polygon–arc topology

Polygons represent area features. A coverage polygon is made up of arc that define the boundary and a label point that links the polygon feature to an attribute record in the coverage PAT. ArcInfo stores polygons topologically as a list of arcs and a label that make up each polygon.

preview

A live view of GIS data in ArcCatalog. You can pan and zoom the preview, query features, and create thumbnail images to store in metadata.

projection

A mathematical formula that transforms feature locations from the earth's curved surface to a map's flat surface. A projected coordinate system employs a projection to transform locations expressed as latitude and longitude values to x,y coordinates. Projections cause distortions in one or more of these spatial properties: distance, area, shape, and direction.

query

A question or request used for selecting features. A query often appears in the form of a statement or logical expression. In ArcMap, a query contains a field, an operator, and a value.

raster

Represents any data source that uses a grid structure to store geographic information. See grid and image.

RDBMS

Relational database management system. A database management system with the ability to access data organized in tabular files that can be related to each other by a common field (item). An RDBMS has the capability to recombine the data items from different files, providing powerful tools for data usage.

scale bar

A map element that shows the map scale graphically.

scanning

The process of capturing data in raster format with a device called a scanner. Some scanners also use software to convert raster data to vector data.

schema

1. The structure or design of a database.

2. The definition of the database. The schema can either be modeled in UML using a CASE tool or defined directly within ArcCatalog using wizard dialog boxes.

SDE

See ArcSDE.

shapefile

A vector data storage format for storing the location, shape, and attributes of geographic features.

simple edge feature

A line that plays a topological role in a network. See also complex edge feature.

simple feature

A feature that implements ESRI Simple Feature. A point, multipoint, line, polyline, or polygon.

simple junction feature

A point feature that plays a topological role in a network. See complex junction feature.

single-user geodatabase

A Personal SDE geodatabase. It can handle a single writer and multiple readers.

snapping

The process of moving a feature to coincide exactly with coordinates of another feature within a specified snapping distance or tolerance.

snapping tolerance

The distance within which the pointer or a feature will snap to another location. If the location being snapped to (vertex, boundary, midpoint, or connection) is within the distance you set, the pointer will automatically snap. For example, if you want to snap a power line to a utility pole and the snapping tolerance is set to 25 pixels, whenever the power line comes within a 25-pixel range of the pole it will automatically snap to it. Snapping tolerance can be measured using either map units or pixels.

spatial analysis

The study of the locations and shapes of geographic features and the relationships between them.

The process of modeling, examining, and interpreting model results. Spatial analysis is useful for evaluating suitability and capability, for estimating and predicting, and for interpreting and understanding. There are four traditional types of spatial analysis: topological overlay and contiguity analysis, surface analysis, linear analysis, and raster analysis.

spatial bookmark

Identifies a particular geographic location that you want to save and refer to later—for example, a study area.

spatial modeling

Analytical procedures applied with a GIS. There are three categories of spatial modeling functions that can be applied to geographic features within a GIS: (1) geometric models, such as calculating the Euclidean distance between features, generating buffers, calculating areas and perimeters, and so on; (2) coincidence models, such as topological overlay; and (3) adjacency models (pathfinding, redistricting, and allocation). All three model categories support operations on spatial data such as points, lines, polygons, TINs, and GRIDs. Functions are organized in a sequence of steps to derive the desired information for analysis. See also model and analysis.

spatial query

See location query.

table of contents

Lists all the data frames and layers on the map.

thumbnail image

A static image of data or a map stored in the metadata. You can create and view thumbnail images for data in ArcCatalog.

TIN

Triangulated irregular network. A surface representation derived from irregularly spaced sample points and breakline features. The TIN dataset includes topological relationships between points and their neighboring triangles. Each sample point has an x,y coordinate and a surface or z-value. These points are connected by edges to form a set of nonoverlapping triangles used to represent the surface. TIN is also called an irregular triangular mesh or an irregular triangular surface model.

toolbar

A set of buttons that you click to carry out common tasks. Toolbars can float in their own window, or you can dock them at the top, bottom, or sides of the main window.

Toolbox tree

Displays ArcToolbox toolsets and tools grouped by functionality.

toolset

A grouping of tools that perform a similar geoprocessing task. Custom toolsets can be created within the My Tools toolset to hold custom tools as well as to group frequently used ArcToolbox tools.

topology

The spatial relationships between connecting or adjacent coverage features (for example, arcs, nodes, polygons, and points). For example, the topology of an arc includes its from- and to-nodes and its left and right polygons. Topological relationships are built from simple elements into complex elements: points (simplest elements), arcs (sets of connected points), areas (sets of connected arcs), and routes (sets of sections, which are arcs or portions of arcs). Redundant data (coordinates) is eliminated because an arc may represent a linear feature, part of the boundary of an area feature, or both. Topology is useful in GIS because many spatial modeling operations do not require coordinates, only topological information. For example, to find an optimal path between two points requires a list of the arcs that connect to each other and the cost to traverse each arc in each direction. Coordinates are only needed for drawing the path after it is calculated.

union

A topological overlay of two polygonal spatial datasets that preserve features that fall within the spatial extent of either input dataset; that is, all features from both coverages are retained. See also intersect and identity.

VBA

Visual Basic for Applications. The embedded programming environment for automating and customizing ESRI end-user applications such as ArcMap and ArcCatalog. It offers the same powerful tools as Visual Basic (VB) in the context of an existing application and is the best option for customizing software that already meets most needs. By contrast, VB is a standalone tool for rapidly creating a special solution from scratch, be it an executable program, COM component, or an ActiveX® control. An application that uses ArcMap or ArcCatalog may require the development of a COM component; consequently, in such instances, VB is the appropriate development environment.

vector model

A representation of the world using points, lines, and areas. Vector models are useful for representing and storing discrete features such as buildings, pipes, or parcel boundaries.

virtual page

The map page, as seen in layout view.

wizard

A tool that leads a user step by step through an unusually long, difficult, or complex task.

zoom

To enlarge and display greater detail of a portion of a geographic dataset.

Index

Vector data
   examples 46
   topological 98
Vector model
   defined 218
   examples 46
   implementations of 46
View (ArcCatalog)
   contents 11
      details 19
      large icons 19
   metadata 11, 19
   preview 11, 19, 75
View (ArcMap)
   data 35, 166
   layout 35, 166
Viewing data in ArcCatalog
   contents 19
   thumbnail image 22
Virtual page
   in Layout view 36, 167
Visibility analysis
   surface tools in ArcToolbox 47
Visual Basic for Applications (VBA)
   programming ArcInfo 24
Volume
   surface tools in ArcToolbox 47

W

Weight
   in suitability model 131
Welcome to ArcInfo 3, 5
WGS84 88
What are coordinate systems? 88
What is a GIS analysis? 60
What is coverage topology? 98
What is next? 43, 210
Windows
   desktop applications 11
   printer driver 42

Wizard
   defined 218
Workspace
   storage of coverages in 51
World Geodetic System of 1984 88

Z

Zoom
   defined 218
   in ArcCatalog 77
   in ArcMap 25, 162
   layout tools 183, 195, 197
   to a bookmarked area 27
   while editing 110